A Year on a Cape Wine Estate

Entertaining

AT HAMILTON RUSSELL VINEYARDS

Wine suggestions by Miguel Chan, certified sommelier, Tsogo Sun

A Year on a Cape Wine Estate
Entertaining
AT HAMILTON RUSSELL VINEYARDS

Olive Hamilton Russell

ontents

Introduction 7

Spring
September 13

Focaccia 14

Squid-ink ravioli filled with goat's cheese in
a lime and shark biltong cream sauce 17

Peppered shoulder of spring lamb with roasted baby
vegetables in a Pinot Noir sauce 20

Rhubarb ice cream with rose meringues
and mini toffee apples 25

October 29

Walker Bay abalone done three ways 31

Chicken breasts baked in a lemon and
anchovy butter sauce 34
Butterbean mash 36
Asparagus purée 36
Fresh asparagus 36

Rose geranium chocolate mousse 41

November 43

Walker Bay octopus served with
three dipping sauces 44

Lemon-baked yellowtail 49
Artichokes with hollandaise sauce 50
Cauliflower soufflé 51

Summer fruits in a white chocolate,
almond and honey sauce 54

Summer
December 59

Gnocchi with prawn and white mussel mayonnaise
garnished with fresh avocado and almonds 61

Roast turkey with sage and orange stuffing,
with cranberry and Pinot Noir sauce
and deep-fried vine leaves 64
Roasted sweet potato chips with chilli and ginger 66

Ginger biscuit ice cream with
cranberry and orange jelly 71

January 73

Chilled cucumber and wild sorrel soup,
garnished with white milkwood berry syrup 75

Walker Bay crayfish with lemon,
ginger and coriander sauce 78

Honey panna cotta with Chardonnay-poached
prickly pears and fresh prickly pears 83

February 85

Ravioli of alikreukel and seaweed in a chilli,
lemongrass and coconut milk broth 86

Kingklip with a parsley crème fraîche sauce 91
Beetroot and cardamom pap with edamame beans 92

Fig and pistachio tart
with Sauvignon Blanc sorbet 96

Autumn

March 103

Mushroom risotto 104

Lime-marinated Cape salmon 108
Salad of rocket, sorrel, courgette, radish
and pine nuts 108
Stuffed courgette flowers 110

Mango and lemon-scented geranium sorbet
on lemon verbena shortbread 115

April 117

Ravioli of venison biltong and mushrooms
in a creamy mushroom sauce 119

Baby sole baked in a creamy lemon-shrimp sauce
topped with capelin caviar 122
Potato, pea and fennel mash 122

Olive oil ice cream with sour fig syrup 129

May 131

Fairfield fallow deer sausage with
porcini pap and porcini cream sauce 132

Franschhoek salmon trout with kaffir lime oil 137
Creamy pink peppercorn and
cashew nut samp 138

Malva pudding
with cape gooseberry custard 140

Winter

June 147

Walker Bay black mussel bunny chow
in a 'kooigoed' sauce 148

Roasted Stellenbosch quails with pancetta,
black olive and honey stuffing 151
Fresh green beans in a sesame dressing 152
Parisienne potatoes with flat-leaf parsley 152

Milk tart in cinnamon phyllo pastry cases
with quince and rosehip cream 155

July 161

Smoked snoek chowder with wild sorrel served with
lemon thyme mini-loaves 163

Pan-fried fillet of beef with
a creamy horseradish sauce 166
Warm salad of multi-coloured chard and red onion 168
Rosemary-skewered roast potatoes 169

Hamilton Russell Vineyards Pinot
Noir-poached pear brûlée tart 172

August 175

Waterblommetjie risotto with bokkoms 176

Breast of guinea fowl with olive and
rosemary tapenade 181
Turnip and parsnip purée 182

Lemon and ginger tartlets flavoured with violets 186

Index 188
Conversion tables 190

Dedication

Hamilton Russell Vineyards

Founded in 1975, with the first wines released in 1981, Hamilton Russell Vineyards is the pioneering
family-run wine Estate in the beautiful Hemel-en-Aarde Valley wine appellation, situated just behind
the seaside resort town of Hermanus, on the shores of Walker Bay, some 120km southeast of Cape Town.
(Hemel-en-Aarde is old Dutch for 'Heaven and Earth'.)
Specialising in producing a single, Estate-grown-and-made Pinot Noir and a single Estate-grown-and-made
Chardonnay, Hamilton Russell Vineyards has developed a significant international reputation for these wines,
which are regarded as being among the very best examples made outside Burgundy,
and world classics in their own right.
The high quality, cool growing conditions of the Hemel-en-Aarde Valley are a function of its close
proximity to the cold Atlantic Ocean; at its closest point, Walker Bay is only 1500 metres away from
Hamilton Russell Vineyards. This cool, strongly maritime and Mediterranean climate, combined with stony,
iron-rich soils that have an extremely high clay-content, has resulted in Pinot Noir and Chardonnay with an
unusually classic style and structure; almost unique in the New World.
The current, second generation, owner, Anthony Hamilton Russell, took over from his father, Tim, in 1991
and bought the business from him in 1994. Hamilton Russell Vineyards has now made more than 30 vintages
of Pinot Noir and Chardonnay from the same unique site, surrounded by nature reserve, close to the
southern tip of Africa and the cold, clean Atlantic.

Introduction

Good food, like good wine, tells a story of place at a point in time. This book is a celebration, through food, of a particular place, the wine estate Hamilton Russell Vineyards, situated in the beautiful Hemel-en-Aarde valley behind the seaside resort town of Hermanus, not far from the southernmost tip of Africa.

The wines of Hamilton Russell Vineyards have developed an international reputation over the course of more than 30 years. As a result, we regularly host visitors from around the world. It has always been our goal to entertain our guests in a way which fits both the place and the particular season of their visit. Just as the appeal of our wines is their ability to reflect the unchanging characteristics of site and soil, while also expressing the particular personality of each vintage, so too we hope that our food expresses the essence of the local environment, with all its historic influences, as well as specific attractions of the season.

As wine enthusiasts with a finite capacity for consumption, we are only too aware of the importance of drinking well. Each indifferent bottle drunk is an opportunity lost. As food enthusiasts, we find that time spent thinking about a meal, its ingredients, its relevance to place and time, adds immeasurably to the pleasures of its consumption. Over the course of our lives, we spend nearly 20 per cent of our waking hours enjoying a meal; some much more and some much less but, as a means of enhancing quality of life, it is worth spending this time well.

Although many of the recipes in this book use ingredients specific to our particular location, we have tried to suggest more widely available substitutes. We are enthusiastic foragers on our Estate, seeking out wild mushrooms and edible plants, and this opportunity is not available to everyone. However, we hope that our philosophy of expressing a particular place through food, and adding further to this by expressing a particular season or month, is something this book promotes and reinforces. The great wines and the great cuisines of the world are invariably founded on a strong aesthetic philosophy. It is within all of us to develop an individual, personally relevant approach to the way we prepare and enjoy our meals. This book communicates ours.

It has often been said that food should feed both the stomach and the eye. It is our belief that when beautifully presented food is relevant to a place of personal meaning and to a particular stage in the cycle of the year, it feeds not only the stomach and the eye, but the spirit as well.

Spring

In the vineyard, the team begins to 'build the harvest'. Nature is on the run, and will be for a while.

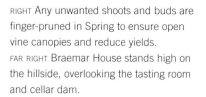

RIGHT Any unwanted shoots and buds are finger-pruned in Spring to ensure open vine canopies and reduce yields.
FAR RIGHT Braemar House stands high on the hillside, overlooking the tasting room and cellar dam.

September

Awakening. The season has turned and Spring has arrived with its promise of all that's beneficial and benign. Some ancient, giant alarm clock has lifted the vines from their deep winter sleep and the first buds green-up the dark cordon arms. Birdsong everywhere. Weavers advertise the quality of their new housing loudly. The herons are back on their rickety perches of carelessly assembled twigs high in the sugar gums and the southern right whales are back from their Antarctic feeding grounds in full force. Walker Bay is alive with them. Some are here to mate and others to calve.

In the vineyards the team begins 'building the harvest'. The goal is to stay on top of things. Nature is on the run and will be for a while. Small unwanted shoots and buds are 'finger pruned' – simply picked off the vines. The cover crop in the rows is mowed again, and then again, with the cuttings serving as mulch for the soil. Shiny, black forktailed drongos follow the mowers, diving for the disturbed insects with dash and courage. Organic plant food is distributed ahead of forecast rain, and a small team is busy tightening wires and repairing trellising.

But it's quiet in the cellar. A time for tasting, checking and analyzing. The wines are slowly growing towards being bottle ready.

Outdoors, it's a carnival of scent; a perfumer's delight. Who could think a 'keurblom' could smell so good? Forget the jasmine and wisteria, there is something extra here, a heady floral spice from before time. It's as though the slightly drab, unprepossessing shrub, wild and ungardened, has saved all year to dazzle in Spring. Economizing on all other senses to focus on the olfactory alone. But if you are prepared to trade scent for sight, the 'rooisewejaartjie' (*Phaenocoma prolifera*) is out on the stony mountain slopes in all its scarlet glory: dark black to washed olive grey-green foliage with almost impossibly vivid dry 'everlasting' flowers. The sugar gum (*Eucalyptus cladocalyx*) forest, established at the turn of the last century, reaches even further for the pure sun, with coppery tops of new growth on old canopies. Flora, and fauna, are sharp and on show.

It's safari season, and well-heeled American, British and German visitors (among others) add an in-depth wine estate visit, or three, to their South African trip. Tastings and lunches are held at home and elsewhere with trade customers and wine enthusiasts. A wine show or two. The pace builds and the pulse quickens.

Focaccia

This is household staple which we love to serve with drinks before the meal.

190g white bread flour

pinch of salt

10g (1 sachet) instant yeast

110–150ml lukewarm water

Hamilton Russell Vineyards
    Extra-virgin Olive Oil

Maldon salt flakes

fresh rosemary leaves, olives, pine
    nuts or cashews, chopped (*see*
    Cook's notes)

Serves 8

1. In a large bowl, sift the flour and salt together. Add the yeast, and stir to combine.
2. Slowly add the water, while mixing with a wooden spoon, ensuring the mixture does not become runny.
3. Knead the mixture until it forms a firm ball. Cover with a tea towel and leave for 30 minutes to prove.
4. Heat the oven to 180°C.
5. Place the dough on a clean, floured surface. Punch down, then roll out as thinly as possible.
6. Grease two baking trays with a little olive oil. Cut the dough to fit the trays.
7. Place the dough on the trays, drizzle with olive oil and sprinkle with Maldon salt.
8. Bake for approximately 15 minutes on the top oven rack, until golden.
9. Remove from the oven, cut into strips or squares, and serve warm, with extra olive oil for dipping.

COOK'S NOTES

- When I serve the focaccia with Sauvignon Blanc, I sprinkle about 2ml (¼t) finely chopped fresh rosemary leaves and 15ml (1T) chopped olives over the dough just before baking. If I serve it with Chardonnay, I use a tablespoon or two of chopped pine nuts or cashews instead.

Squid-ink ravioli filled with goat's cheese
in a lime and shark biltong cream sauce

The zesty freshness of lime, together with the salty savouriness of the shark biltong, balances the richness of the goat's cheese and cream delightfully.

Squid-ink ravioli

300g cake flour, sifted
100g semolina, sifted
4 eggs
5ml (1t) squid ink (*see* Cook's notes)
160g chevin-style goat's cheese, crumbled

Lime and shark biltong cream sauce

1 litre (4 cups) fresh cream
30ml (2T) powdered shark biltong (*see* Cook's notes)
15ml (1T) fresh lime juice
3ml (½t) lime rind, freshly grated
5ml (1t) rice vinegar
lavender flowers, for garnish

Serves 8

Squid-ink ravioli

1. Place the cake flour, semolina, eggs and squid ink in the bowl of an electric mixer.
2. Using the dough hook, mix on medium speed until an homogenous mix has been achieved.
3. Still using the mixer, knead the dough until it becomes smooth and forms a firm ball. It should not be sticky; if it is, add a little extra semolina. (If you can't knead the dough into a firm ball in the mixer, tip the dough onto a floured work surface and knead by hand.)
4. When the dough stops sticking to the bowl or the work surface, shape it into three or four fist-sized balls and tightly wrap each one in clingfilm.
5. Leave to stand at room temperature for about 30 minutes, to allow the gluten to relax. (Don't leave it for much longer than 30 minutes.)

Shaping, assembling and cooking the ravioli
See pages 86–87.

1. Place half a teaspoon of crumbled chevin on half of the ravioli cut-outs, top with the other half and seal. Cook as indicated on page 87.

Lime and shark biltong cream sauce

1. Heat the cream in a small saucepan.
2. Bring to the boil, simmer for about 5 minutes, then add the other ingredients.
3. Lower the heat and simmer for 8–10 minutes, until the sauce starts to thicken slightly.

To serve
Arrange 6–8 pockets of ravioli per plate and spoon over some warm sauce. Garnish with lavender flowers and serve immediately.

COOK'S NOTES

- Shark biltong is very savoury, so you only need a small quantity. Most fish merchants stock strips of shark biltong. Use a large knife to chop the strips to a fine powder. If you can't get shark biltong, substitute two or three finely chopped anchovy fillets.
- Squid ink can be obtained from specialist seafood suppliers or Asian food importers. It is usually sold in small sachets; 5ml (1t) is the equivalent of two sachets, depending on the brand.
- **To make the pasta dough by hand:** Place the flour in a mound on a clean work surface. Make a well in centre and crack in the eggs, then use a fork to slowly mix the eggs into the flour. Once the egg and flour mixture is combined, start kneading, and follow the method above.
- Ravioli freezes very well, so make it in advance and store in the freezer for up to one month. Layer the ravioli between sheets of baking paper or wax paper, making sure the edges do not touch. Seal in an airtight container. Cook from frozen, allowing an extra minute of cooking time.

WINE SUGGESTIONS

A classic dish bursting with flavour. It needs a ripe, floral yet minerally white wine, preferably a single variety, to highlight the saltiness of the goat's cheese and stand up to the robustness of the shark biltong.

- Sauvignon Blanc from Walker Bay, Western Cape.
- Albariño from high altitude vineyards in the Rias Baixas, Galicia, northwestern Spain.
- Assyrtiko from Santorini, Aegean Islands, Greece.

With over 40 hectares of nature reserve, Hamilton Russell Vineyards is more than just a wine estate.

LEFT Yellow wachendorfia and white arum lilies grow freely in wetland bordering the paddock.
RIGHT Garden sage flowers (*Salvia officinalis*).

LEFT Chincherinchee (*Ornithogalum thyrsoides*).
RIGHT 'Rooisewejaartjie' or false everlasting (*Phaenocoma prolifera*).

Peppered shoulder of spring lamb
with roasted baby vegetables, in a Pinot Noir sauce

What could be more delicious than lamb and vegetables roasted in the earthy, aromatic juices of a young Pinot Noir? This is an ideal dinner party dish, as the meat and vegetables can be left to cook in the oven while you mingle with your guests.

800g baby beetroot, peeled and halved
700g baby potatoes, peeled
2kg shoulder of lamb (*see* Cook's notes)
60ml (4T) black peppercorns, crushed
500ml (2 cups) Hamilton Russell Vineyards
    Pinot Noir, current vintage
300g baby carrots, peeled
200g baby fennel, rinsed and trimmed
200g baby leeks, rinsed and trimmed
Hamilton Russell Vineyards Extra-virgin Olive Oil,
    to drizzle
15ml (1T) cornflour (Maizena)
45ml (3T) water

Serves 8

1. Preheat the oven to 180°C.
2. Bring a saucepan of lightly salted cold water to the boil. Add the beetroot and potatoes and boil together for 15 minutes. Remove from heat and leave to stand for 15 minutes to allow the potatoes to colour, then drain and set aside.
3. Place the lamb in a roasting pan, fat side up, score the fat and rub with crushed peppercorns.
4. Pour half of the wine around the lamb, and roast uncovered for 110 minutes (*see* Cook's notes).
5. Place all the vegetables around the lamb. Drizzle with olive oil and pour the rest of the wine over the lamb and vegetables. Roast for another 10 minutes.
6. Cover the dish with foil and roast for a further 35 minutes.
7. Remove the lamb and vegetables from the pan, cover with foil and leave to rest for 10 minutes.
8. While the meat is resting, pour the pan juices into a small saucepan.
9. Dissolve the cornflour in the water and add to the juices in the saucepan. Heat over medium heat for 10 minutes, while stirring. Keep warm until required.

To serve
Carve the meat and drizzle the sauce over. Serve with the vegetables, tossed in a little olive oil and sprinkled with flaked salt.

COOK'S NOTES
- About 2kg of lamb shoulder on the bone should be enough for 8 people. Most lamb shoulders weigh around 1kg, so use two shoulders for this recipe. You should be able to fit both into a roasting pan; if not, use two pans and divide the vegetables between them.
- If your lamb shoulder weighs more (or less) than 2kg, adjust the timing as follows: roast uncovered for 25 minutes for every 500g, plus an extra 25 minutes covered with foil.
- You can use any young dry red wine for cooking. For a special occasion, go for the best quality wine you can afford; this dish is worth it.

WINE SUGGESTIONS
Spring lamb is delicate in texture. In this dish, the combination of a peppery crust and well-flavoured vegetables requires a structured, full-bodied red wine to highlight their earthy elements. When wine is used in a recipe, a good rule of thumb is to serve the same type of wine that the dish is cooked with. For this dish, Pinot Noir is perfect.
- Hemel en Aarde Pinot Noir from a riper year (preferably with 3–5 years bottle age).
- Californian Pinot Noir from the cool-climate Carneros region.
- From Burgundy, choose Pommard from a reputable domaine. Seek wines from Premier Cru vineyards such as Les Rugiens, Les Epénots (including Clos des Epéneaux) and Pézérolles, with at least 6–8 years bottle age.

Rhubarb ice cream
with rose meringues and mini toffee apples

The soft, tart ice cream, fragrant chewy meringues and crisp, sweet mini toffee apples complement one another superbly.

Rhubarb ice cream

540g fresh rhubarb stalks, rinsed
  and trimmed
80g castor sugar
1 litre (4 cups) fresh cream
8 egg yolks (reserve the whites for
  the meringue)
200g castor sugar
2ml (¼t) vanilla paste

Rose meringues

8 egg whites (reserve the yolks for
  the rhubarb ice cream)
1ml (⅛t) salt
600g castor sugar
200g icing sugar
20ml (4t) rose water
2ml (¼t) pink food colouring

Rhubarb syrup

250g fresh rhubarb stalks, rinsed
  and trimmed
50g castor sugar

Serves 8

Rhubarb ice cream

1. Peel the rhubarb stalks carefully, removing all the stringy bits. Chop each stalk into 4–5 pieces and place in a shallow bowl. Sprinkle with castor sugar and leave to stand for 1½ hours, stirring every 30 minutes.
2. Transfer the rhubarb to a medium saucepan and heat over low heat for 5 minutes, stirring occasionally, to prevent it from sticking.
3. Add the cream and heat slowly to just below boiling point, stirring continuously.
4. Remove from the heat, cover and leave to infuse for 30 minutes.
5. In a separate bowl, use an electric beater to whisk the egg yolks, castor sugar and vanilla paste together until thick and pale yellow (this should take about 5 minutes).
6. Strain the cream (retaining the rhubarb) and add to the egg mixture, while whisking.
7. Scoop the rhubarb solids into a liquidizer and purée. Strain through a sieve, pressing down to extract all the liquid. Discard the solids and add the purée to the cream-egg mixture.
8. Return the custard mixture to a clean pot and heat slowly, stirring continuously. When the mixture coats the back of a spoon, remove the pot from the heat. Do not let it boil.
9. Transfer the custard to a metal bowl and immerse in an ice bath to stop it cooking any further. Stir occasionally until cooled (this will take about 15 minutes), then transfer to an ice cream machine to churn and freeze.

Rose meringues

1. Preheat the oven to 150ºC.
2. Whisk the egg whites, with a pinch of salt in an electric mixer, on medium speed, until they form stiff peaks.
3. Sift together the castor sugar and icing sugar.
4. With the mixer running, add the sugars one tablespoon at a time, making sure the meringue returns to stiff peaks before adding more sugar. Add the rose water and just a drop or two of food colouring.
5. With the mixer on the highest setting, whisk for 8–10 minutes, until the mixture is glossy.
6. Line a baking tray (± 26 x 37cm) with baking paper. Spoon the meringue onto the paper and shape into a rectangle using the back of a spoon. Make swirls around the edges to raise them.
7. Bake for 60 minutes then turn the heat off and leave the meringue in the oven, with the door ajar, until it has cooled completely.

Rhubarb syrup

1. Peel the rhubarb stalks carefully, removing all the stringy bits. Chop each stalk into four to five pieces and place in a shallow bowl.
2. Sprinkle with castor sugar and leave to stand for 1½ hours, stirring every 30 minutes.
3. Transfer to a heavy based saucepan and heat slowly, to melt the sugar. Boil over a low heat for 5 minutes, then strain, retaining both the syrup and the solids.
4. Scoop the rhubarb solids into a liquidizer, purée and strain, retaining the liquid.
5. Add the strained liquid to the syrup and return to a clean saucepan. Simmer over a medium heat for 15–20 minutes until the syrup is a light golden colour. Remove the saucepan from the heat and only use once the syrup stops bubbling.

For Mini toffee apples, Cook's notes and Wine suggestions, see page 27.

Mini toffee apples

1 can baby apples, drained (*see*
  Cook's notes)
225g demerara (golden) sugar
100ml water
3ml (½t) vinegar
30ml (2T) glucose syrup
25g (2T) butter
3ml (½t) red food colouring

1. Line a baking tray with greaseproof paper and spray the paper with non-stick cooking spray.
2. Dry each apple carefully and set aside. (If the apples are wet, the syrup will crystallize.)
3. Place the sugar and water in a saucepan and dissolve over a medium heat.
4. Stir in the vinegar, glucose syrup, butter and red food colouring.
5. Bring to the boil and cook, without stirring, until it reaches hard-ball stage (138°C on a sugar thermometer, or test by dropping a little syrup into a glass of cold water; if it hardens into a ball, the syrup is ready).
6. When the syrup is ready, dip the apples, one by one. Using metal tongs, hold the stem and swirl each apple around in the syrup until it is well coated. Let the excess syrup drip off over the pot before placing the apple on the baking tray to cool and harden. (Take care, as hot syrup can burn!)

To serve

Remove the rhubarb ice cream from the freezer about 10 minutes prior to serving, to soften a little and make it easier to scoop. Place the meringue on a serving platter, and spoon scoops of ice cream onto the meringue, scatter the toffee apples on top and drizzle with the rhubarb syrup. Serve immediately.

COOK'S NOTES

*   Make the ice cream in advance and freeze until required.
*   You can prepare the rhubarb for the syrup in advance, but make the syrup just before serving.
*   Ensure the bowl used for whisking the egg whites is spotlessly clean, with no traces of any grease or fat, egg yolks or shells.
*   To test whether the meringue mixture has been whisked properly, rub a little between your fingers; when you can't feel the granular texture of the sugar anymore, it is done.
*   If you can, leave the meringue in the oven overnight to dry out.
*   A 213g can of baby apples should give you about 16 apples. The toffee apples can be made a day ahead and stored in airtight container. (In very hot weather, store them in the fridge.)
*   Be extremely careful when making the toffee apples, as the syrup gets very hot.

WINE SUGGESTIONS

Rhubarb and roses are the dominant flavours in this dessert. You need a wine that is not too sweet; a late harvest style will be ideal.

*   Late harvest style from Paarl, Western Cape.
*   Vendange Tardive or Selection de Grains Nobles Gewürztraminer from Alsace.

ABOVE Hives set amongst the fynbos provide dark, deep-flavoured, fragrant honey.
RIGHT The blue crane, which is endemic to the Western Cape, is South Africa's national bird.
FAR RIGHT Pincushions (*Leucospermum* spp.) grow freely in the fynbos reserve behind the house.

October

It's been a cool Spring and now at least the feel of Summer is in the air from time to time. The ground is drying out and surface run-off slows and stops. The soil is ready to hold more water and rewards a rain shower with a grateful, earthy smell. The flocks of guineafowl have broken up and partnered off – complicit couples everywhere – and the resident pair of blue cranes is back in the open field of rye, which is resting and building structure prior to re-planting with new vines. If the cranes can outwit the whitenecked ravens they may well raise two chicks again this year. The first gorgeous bowls of hybrid tea roses from the garden appear in the house. The fires are unlikely to be lit again for a while.

The buds in the vineyard have developed into much larger shoots and 'suckering' is underway. Thorough suckering is a crucial activity for quality and there is always an urgency to stay on top of the season's ebullience. With hands and secateurs, unwanted shoots are cut or broken off. It is important that the canopies are not too dense and that the grape yield is in balance with the vine. You can see bunches on the bearing shoots, but they are small and fragile, still just a promise which may be broken. Elsewhere a team is busy clearing the last standing invasive alien vegetation from the wetland, but they know they will be back. There always seems to be something left to seed a further invasion. This battle has been won though, and the wetland is so much cleaner than before.

Creamy green-white flowers open on some of the olive trees around the manor house. The yields are tiny and the traditionally planted and pruned, unirrigated grove reminds us, once again, that it is passion, not profit, that drives its tending.

If you haven't had a close look at a pincushion protea (*Leucospermum* spp.) you must. Such beautifully designed flower heads, like a colourful, carefully teased hairstyle. The rattle-dry everlasting 'sewejaartjies' (*Syncarpha vestita*) form brilliant-white clumps in the recently burned hillside fynbos. Their nickname, 'Cape snow', describes them well; like drifts left in the high mountains on a dark slope in the late Spring. There's a profusion of flowers: shell-pink watsonias, wachendorfias yellowing up the wetlands, and the pelargoniums, the Cape's gift to the world. White, scarlet, purple, pink. There are so many indigenous to the area.

We are entertaining a lot more now, but keep up our regular tastings of wines from around the world alongside our own. We attend a wine show in Johannesburg and another in New York. We pay a quick visit to longstanding customers in Boston and host a few tastings there. We are testing our legs for the full-on season ahead.

Walker Bay abalone
done three ways

Abalone is synonymous with Walker Bay. Known locally as 'perlemoen' or 'pearlies', they are all but extinct in the wild these days, but locally farmed, frozen abalone is available from specialist seafood suppliers. For this recipe, you need 600g of abalone meat.

Deep-fried abalone

4 eggs
280g flour, sifted
500ml (2 cups) canola oil
200g abalone, thinly sliced
60g basil leaves, rinsed

Steamed abalone

1 litre (4 cups) water
2 lemons, quartered
200g abalone, thinly sliced
160ml (⅔ cup) Japanese
   mayonnaise (*see* Cook's notes)
30ml (2T) black seaweed caviar
30ml (2T) pink seaweed caviar (*see*
  Cook's notes)
pinch of salt
250ml (1 cup) canola oil
50g dill, rinsed and dried well

Pan-fried abalone

200g abalone, thinly sliced
15ml (1T) finely chopped garlic
15ml (1T) fresh lemon juice
10ml (2t) finely grated lemon rind
125ml (½ cup) Hamilton Russell
  Vineyards Extra-virgin Olive Oil
100g butter
60g rocket, rinsed

Serves 8

Deep-fried abalone

1. Beat the eggs, add the flour and mix to form a batter.
2. Heat the oil in a large frying pan.
3. Dip the abalone slices in the batter, allowing any excess batter to drip off. Fry in batches in the hot oil until golden brown (about 1–2 minutes per side), making sure the slices remain separate. Drain on paper towel and keep warm in the oven. Serve hot on a bed of fresh basil leaves.

Steamed abalone

1. In a wok or saucepan, bring 1 litre of water to the boil and add the lemon quarters.
2. Arrange the abalone slices in a bamboo steamer. Steam for 5–10 minutes, until the edge of the meat feels firm and starts curling. Remove from the heat.
3. Combine the mayonnaise, seaweed caviars and salt and fold in the abelone slices.
4. Just before serving, heat the oil in a pan, and fry the sprigs of dill until crispy.
5. Spread the fried dill on a serving platter and top with the dressed abalone.

Pan-fried abalone

1. Combine the abalone with the garlic, lemon juice and lemon rind.
2. Heat the olive oil and butter in a large frying pan. Fry the abalone for 3–5 minutes (in batches if necessary), until the garlic is golden and the abalone starts to crisp.
3. Remove from the pan and keep warm. Serve hot on a bed of rocket.

To serve

Arrange slices of the abalone on individual plates or group them on one large platter.

COOK'S NOTES

- I use a Parma ham slicer to slice the abalone very thinly (± 2mm thick); alternatively, use a very sharp knife.
- Smaller abalone are more tender than the larger ones. If you can only get large abalone, it is important to tenderize the meat before cooking. Do this by arranging the slices on a wooden chopping board, covering them with cling wrap and then pounding them with a wooden meat mallet.
- Dry the dill well before frying in the hot oil. The sprigs will be ready when the oil stops sizzling.
- Japanese mayonnaise is sold locally under the Kewpie brand. Look for it in the oriental section of the supermarket or at specialist suppliers.
- Abalone poaching is rife along parts of the Cape coast, and there are strict limits on recreational harvesting, so make sure you buy seafood only from a legitimate supplier.
- Seaweed (vegetarian) caviar is a healthier and more environmentally friendly option than traditional caviar. It comes in red (pink), black and 'wasabi green' versions and can be used in both hot and cold dishes. It is available from good supermarkets and specialist suppliers.

WINE SUGGESTIONS

Abalone is a delicacy with a meaty texture, full of flavour and briny. This dish needs a tangy, zesty minerally white wine to cut through the robust flavour of Japanese mayonnaise, garlic and seaweed caviar.

- Subtly oaked Semillon from the Cape Peninsula, Western Cape.
- Gavi di Gavi, a refreshing wine from Piedmont, Italy.
- Grüner Veltliner, a food-friendly wine from Wachau, Kamptal or Kremstal districts, Austria.

Everlasting 'sewejaartjies' (*Syncarpha vestita*) form brilliant-white clumps in the hillside fynbos. Their nickname, 'Cape snow', describes them well; like drifts left in the high mountains on a dark slope in the late Spring.

LEFT Everlastings, known as 'sewejaartjies' or Cape snow (*Syncarpha vestita*), grow on the rocky slopes.
RIGHT Perlemoen, or abalone, are found in the cold waters of Walker Bay.

LEFT Small fragile bunches of grapes are starting to develop their tiny fruits.
RIGHT The 'Athene' rose was named in honour of Anthony's mother on her 60th birthday.

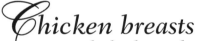hicken breasts
baked in a lemon and anchovy butter sauce

I like to serve this with a creamy butterbean mash, flavoured with lemon thyme, and a duo of the new season's asparagus.

8 skinless deboned chicken breasts
8 anchovy fillets
3ml (½t) anchovy oil (*see* Cook's notes)
80ml (5T) fresh lemon juice
60g butter (*see* Cook's notes)
10ml (2t) finely grated lemon rind
35g capers (there is no need to rinse these)
pinch of white pepper
anchovy fillets, for garnish
flat-leaf parsley, for garnish

Serves 8

1. Preheat the oven to 180°C.
2. Line a roasting pan with foil (shiny side facing), and arrange the chicken breasts on top.
3. Mash the anchovy fillets in a pestle and mortar, adding the anchovy oil.
4. Combine the mashed anchovy fillets with the lemon juice and pour over the chicken.
5. Cut the butter into pieces and scatter over the chicken, together with the lemon rind, capers and a dash of white pepper.
6. Cover with another sheet of foil, fold the edges over to seal the parcel, and bake for 30 minutes.

To serve
Spoon some cooking juices over the chicken breasts. Garnish each one with an extra anchovy fillet, a few capers and a sprig of flat-leaf parsley.

COOK'S NOTES
- Use some of the oil from the jar or tin of anchovies.
- For handy measuring, one quarter of a 250g block of butter is ±60g.
- Making a foil parcel seals in the juices, helping to keep the breasts moist and succulent.

WINE SUGGESTIONS
A simple dish, highlighted by the lemons, anchovies, butter and salt. A herbal, lemony, steely dry, yet powerful and complex white wine will cut through all these flavours, and the asparagus too.
- Chenin Blanc from Paarl in the Western Cape.
- Savennieres from the Anjou region in the Loire valley, France. Seek out La Coulee de Serrant or La Roche aux Moines vineyards.
- Grüner Veltliner from Wachau, Kamptal or Kremstal, Austria.

For Butterbean mash, Asparagus purée and Fresh asparagus, see page 36.

Butterbean mash

4 cans butterbeans, drained
   and rinsed
80ml fresh cream
60g butter
5ml (1t) lemon thyme leaves, rinsed
   (*see* Cook's notes)
2ml (¼t) lemon pepper
5ml (1t) vegetable stock powder

1. Place the rinsed and drained butterbeans in a medium saucepan.
2. Add the cream and mash the butterbeans, using a hand-held blender. The end result should be
    a smooth-textured mash.
3. Add all the other ingredients, and heat over medium heat while stirring.
    Serve hot.

COOK'S NOTES
*   Use four 410g cans of butterbeans, or adjust as necessary to get ±1.6kg of butterbeans.
*   Instead of fresh lemon thyme leaves, use 2ml (¼t) of dried thyme and 3ml (½t) finely grated lemon rind.

Asparagus purée

2 litres (8 cups) chicken stock
750g green asparagus spears,
   rinsed and trimmed
40g butter, cut into cubes
pinch of salt
15ml (1T) fresh lemon juice
3ml (½t) grated lemon rind

1. Bring the stock to the boil in a medium saucepan.
2. Add the asparagus spears and cook for 5–7 minutes, just until tender but still bright green.
3. Drain, refresh and return to the pot.
4. Add the butter, salt, lemon juice and lemon rind and purée, using a hand-held blender, until smooth.
    Serve hot. (This can be made ahead and reheated before serving.)

Fresh asparagus

1 litre (4 cups) chicken stock
200g mini green asparagus spears,
   rinsed and trimmed

1. Bring the stock to the boil in a medium saucepan.
2. Add the asparagus spears and cook for 5–7 minutes until tender, but still bright green.
3. Drain and serve hot.

To serve
Serve with Chicken breasts baked in a lemon and anchovy butter sauce, *see* page 34.

Rose geranium chocolate mousse

When I make this recipe, I use locally made artisanal chocolate, and petals from a rose named after my mother-in-law, Athene, but it will taste just as good made with readily available chocolate and roses from your own garden.

Chocolate mousse

90g DV Madagascar (70% cacao) Chocolate (*see* Cook's notes)
100g Von Geusau Rose Geranium Chocolate (*see* Cook's notes)
15ml (1T) full-cream milk
1 egg yolk, lightly beaten
35ml (2½T) castor sugar
30ml (2T) icing sugar
5 egg whites
pinch of salt

Candied rose petals

8 'Athene' rose petals (*see* Cook's notes)
1 egg white
100g castor sugar

Chocolate mousse

1. Break the chocolate into small pieces. Place in a metal bowl over simmering water and allow to melt, stirring constantly. Do not allow the base of the bowl to touch the water.
2. Once melted, add the milk and mix well, using a wire whisk.
3. Remove the bowl from the heat and whisk in the beaten egg yolk. Allow to cool.
4. Sift the castor sugar and icing sugar together.
5. In a separate, clean bowl, whisk the egg whites with a pinch of salt until they form soft peaks, then add the sugars, a spoonful at a time.
6. Whisk a quarter of the egg whites into the melted chocolate until well combined, then carefully fold in the remaining egg whites, taking care not to overmix.
7. Pour into small ramekins or cups and chill for at least 2 hours, or overnight.

Candied rose petals

1. Carefully rinse and dry the rose petals.
2. Lightly beat the egg white with a fork.
3. Brush both sides of each rose petal with the egg white, and dip in the castor sugar to coat.
4. Place on a drying rack and leave overnight to harden.

To serve

Top each portion of chocolate mousse with a candied rose petal.

COOK'S NOTES

- The 'Athene' rose is white, but any white or pale pink rose will do. It is important to only use petals from roses that have not been sprayed with any insecticide or chemicals.
- DV Artisan Chocolate is made in Paarl, in the Western Cape. They produce five different 'chocolates of origin' using cacao beans from Trinidad, Venezuela and São Tomé, an island off the west coast of Africa. My choice for this recipe is the DV 70% Cacao bar, which is made from beans grown in the remote Sambirano Valley in Madagascar.
- Von Geusau Chocolates are made in Greyton, in the Western Cape. The range includes a number of interesting flavours, including a very popular chilli chocolate. If you can't source Rose Geranium chocolate, substitute with 100g top quality plain (milk) chocolate and 6 drops of rose water.
- To achieve a light-textured mousse, fold the whisked egg whites into the chocolate very gently, retaining as much air as possible.

WINE SUGGESTIONS

The bold combination of flavours from the 70% Cacao chocolate and the Rose Geranium chocolate require a fortified sweet red wine to stand up to their dominance.
- Red Muscadel, a fortified wine from South Africa's Breede River Valley.
- Banyuls, a Grenache-based fortified wine from Roussillon, southern France.

In the vineyards, flowering is a critical time, and we hope for mild weather or, at least, no strong winds.

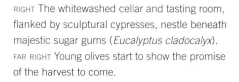

RIGHT The whitewashed cellar and tasting room, flanked by sculptural cypresses, nestle beneath majestic sugar gums (*Eucalyptus cladocalyx*). FAR RIGHT Young olives start to show the promise of the harvest to come.

November

Nature's seemingly unrestrained gathering of pace matures into a steadier tempo. The cover crop in the rows and the resting fields turns a bright khaki hue. The baboon troop watches, waits and descends from the fynbos reserve to feast on the nutritious 'korog' (triticale) seed. The vines grow on, but now the harvest begins to form in earnest with flowering (such a delicate, almost hidden scent and small cream flowers) and berry set. It's a critical time and we hope for mild weather, or at least no excessive winds. The tucking and suckering of vine shoots is nearing an end.

Towards the middle of the month, after carefully tasting through the 'lots', the Chardonnay is considered ready to come out of the barrel. The near complete wine is assembled in large stainless steel tanks for one single wine, a multilayered composite of numerous different personalities. Here it will rest a while to integrate and settle prior to bottling. We have learned greatly from our tastings of the different components and experimental lots. Our Pinot Noir is nearing its time too, but needs perhaps another month in wood. Its wonderful spice and wild berry perfume augers well.

Each month, the fynbos stages a different show: colours, costumes and all. This month, the pale, lemon-yellow everlastings (*Edmondia sesamoides*) make their debut in the shallow, white, sandy soils of the hilltops. Their delicate curved stems and dry crisp heads are grouped in low bunches, like something you could imagine waving gently back and forth in a tidal pool. The last fire cleared their stage and it's their turn to use it. Around them the 'bergstompie' bushes (*Nebelia paleacea*) brighten up the slopes like well-fluffed white cushions. On the farm, the cork oaks are in flower and pushing new growth, while nearby in the paddock the magnolia trees are sporting their enormous, headily scented, easily bruised white flowers. It is an ancient plant, little changed for many millions of years. Pelicans wheeling slowly around against the mountain in a carefully chosen thermal, gaining height and then riding a high current at great speed towards the next lagoon, are a magnificent sight.

It's not just friends and customers who begin to come en masse. Its snake season too. They are on the move and our count of the poisonous ones is seven puff adders around the buildings, a few Cape cobras, a boomslang or two and some berg adders.

Entertainment gathers pace as we host wine writers, distributors, sommeliers, wine clubs, restaurateurs and friends from several countries. There is a tasting and lunch on more days than not, two trips to Johannesburg and a few wine functions. We are getting fit for the season proper. And at night, the late peace of the fierynecked nightjar's distinct call. Clear and pure in the cool, moisture-laden air.

Walker Bay octopus
served with three dipping sauces

Octopus is a hugely underrated, very versatile seafood, and there are many delicious ways to enjoy it. I like to serve this dish with dipping sauces, including my own version of Romesco, a Spanish sauce made from roasted red peppers, tomatoes and almonds, that traditionally accompanies seafood. Serve the sauces in individual bowls or pass around a larger bowl for guests to help themselves.

Octopus

250g fresh octopus tentacles
(*see* Cook's notes)
2–4 litres salted water (*see*
Cook's notes)

Romesco-inspired sauce

1 large red pepper
1 large yellow pepper
1 medium tomato, peeled,
deseeded and chopped
70g almonds, blanched and
skinned (*see* Cook's notes)
2 cloves garlic, roasted (*see* Cook's
notes)
1ml (⅛t) crushed dried chilli flakes
3ml (½t) smoked paprika
60ml (¼ cup) red wine vinegar
125ml (½ cup) Hamilton Russell
Vineyards Extra-virgin Olive Oil,
plus extra, for sautéeing

Sesame and ginger vinaigrette

60ml (¼ cup) sesame oil
60ml (¼ cup) dark soy sauce
125ml (½ cup) rice vinegar
15ml (2½t) pickled ginger,
finely chopped
60ml (¼ cup) Hamilton Russell
Vineyards Extra-virgin Olive Oil
160ml (⅔ cup) mirin (*see*
Cook's notes)
2ml (¼t) fish sauce

Green olive vinaigrette

50g green olives, pitted
75ml (5T) white wine vinegar
125ml (½ cup) Hamilton Russell
Vineyards Extra-virgin Olive Oil
2ml (¼t) flaked salt
30ml (2T) fresh lime juice
15ml (1T) grated lime rind

Octopus

1. In a large saucepan, bring the salted water to the boil. Slowly lower the tentacles into the boiling water to avoid a sudden drop in temperature.
2. Partially cover the pot and simmer for about 30–40 minutes, on low to medium heat. If the water temperature is too high the skin will break and come off.
3. Once cooked, turn the heat off and leave the tentacles to cool in the water (this will help to make the meat even more tender).
4. Once cooled, drain the tentacles and slice them into very thin slices.

Romesco-inspired sauce

1. To roast the peppers, halve them and remove the seeds and white veins. Place under a hot grill for 5–7 minutes until black blisters form on the skin. Put the peppers into a plastic bag (or a bowl covered with clingfilm) and leave for about 10 minutes to sweat, then rub off the skins and slice the flesh into strips.
2. Sauté the tomato in a little olive oil for about 4–5 minutes, until soft.
3. Place the roasted peppers, tomato, almonds, roasted garlic, chilli flakes and paprika into a food processor and blend to a thick purée.
4. With the motor running, slowly drizzle in the vinegar and olive oil. Decant into a suitable bowl, cover and chill until needed.
This will keep for up to a week in the fridge in a sealed container.

Sesame and ginger vinaigrette

1. In a small bowl, whisk all the ingredients together, using a small wire whisk.
Set aside until required.

Green olive vinaigrette

1. Slice the olives into thin rounds.
2. In a small bowl, whisk together the vinegar, olive oil, salt, lime juice and rind.
3. Add the olive slices and set aside until required.

To serve

Arrange slices of octopus tentacles on a platter or on individual serving boards, and serve with the trio of dipping sauces.

COOK'S NOTES

- Octopus bought from a good fish counter or seafood supplier should be properly cleaned, with the slime removed, but if you catch the octopus yourself, you will need to prepare it. I find the following technique works best. It comes from *Nobu the Cookbook*, based on recipes from renowned chef Nobu Matsuhisa. Kill the octopus in the swiftest and most 'humane' way possible, by inserting your knife horizontally into the space between the eyes, and slicing from side to side (to sever the nervous system). Using a sharp knife, cut around the beak to remove it, and turn the head inside out. Remove the ink sac, innards and eggs, if any are present. Rinse well under cold running water. Remove excess sinews. Turn the head back the right way, and place in an unglazed earthenware mixing bowl. Rub the octopus around the bowl. The sliminess will appear as small white bubbles, almost resembling egg white. Continue rubbing the octopus around the bowl for 5–10 minutes, until all the sliminess and sand has been removed. Rinse very well. If it still feels slimy, repeat.
- To cook the octopus, add 30g of salt per litre of cold water (3% salted water).
- To roast garlic, place the unpeeled cloves on a baking tray, drizzle over 2ml (¼t) olive oil and roast for 20 minutes at 180°C until soft and caramelized. Squeeze the pulp from the skins.
- Blanch almonds by soaking them in boiling water for 1 minute and then rubbing the skins off between your thumb and forefinger.
- Mirin is a sweet Japanese rice wine. It is available from good delicatessans, supermarkets and oriental food suppliers. If you can't find it, substitute with medium cream sherry.

- Most versions of Romesco sauce include toasted breadcrumbs, but I leave them out and add more olive oil instead. I also like the flavour that comes from combining red and yellow peppers.
- As this recipe uses only a few tentacles from an octopus, cut the remaining tentacles and the head into bite-sized pieces and use them in a seafood salad or to make ceviche.

WINE SUGGESTIONS

This tapas-style boiled octopus requires an elegant, textured and juicy white blend, or a lemony, spicy and floral single varietal to complement the three dipping sauces.

- Unoaked white blend with some light bottle ageing, from Walker Bay in the Western Cape.
- Robola, an aromatic wine from the island of Cephalonia, Greece.

At this time of the year, local and overseas visitors begin to arrive in greater numbers.

LEFT Sharing the current vintage of Chardonnay with an overseas visitor.
RIGHT The carefully locked underground wine library holds a collection of past vintages for research.

LEFT Relaxing with a glass of Chardonnay, Olive is joined by Horrocks, the Great Dane.
RIGHT The tasting room welcomes visitors six days a week.

Lemon-baked yellowtail

Yellowtail are fast, predatory gamefish that live in the cold Atlantic waters off the Cape coast. During the annual sardine run, they migrate towards the east coast to feast on the sardines. The flesh is firm and full flavoured, but it can easily become dry if even slightly overcooked. I like to serve this with artichokes dressed with hollandaise sauce and individual cauliflower soufflés.

2kg fresh whole yellowtail, head and tail intact
60ml (¼ cup) Hamilton Russell Vineyards Extra-virgin Olive Oil
60ml (¼ cup) fresh lemon juice
3ml (½t) flaked salt
2ml (¼t) freshly ground black pepper
4 sprigs fresh rosemary
30ml (2T) chopped fennel (bulbs and fronds)
1 lemon, sliced into rounds
fresh fennel or other fresh herbs, for garnish

Serves 8

1. Preheat the oven to 200°C.
2. Rub the inside of the fish with 30ml (2T) olive oil.
3. Drizzle the lemon juice over the flesh and season with salt and pepper.
4. Place the rosemary, fennel and lemon slices inside the fish.
5. Place the fish on a lightly greased baking tray and rub the skin with the rest of the olive oil.
6. Bake for 30–40 minutes, until cooked.

To serve
Garnish with fresh fennel or other fresh herbs.

COOK'S NOTES
- Instead of fresh yellowtail (*Seriola* spp., also known as amberjack), you can use any similar firm-fleshed fish, such as Cape salmon (geelbek), kabeljou (kob) or swordfish.
- My fail-safe method to test whether fish is cooked is to insert a sharp knife into the thickest part of the flesh for 5 seconds. If the knife comes out hot to the touch, the fish is cooked.
- A whole fish is always tasty when cooked on an open fire.

WINE SUGGESTIONS
This full-textured fish with its bold vegetable accompaniments requires a medium-bodied, juicy, crisp red wine (chilled to 10–12°C) to tame the artichokes and provide a natural, sour-cherry acidity that will cut through the richness of the cauliflower soufflé and the hollandaise sauce.
- Klein River Sangiovese, Western Cape.
- Morellino di Scansano, from Tuscany, Italy.
- Chinon or Saumur Champigny from Loire Valley, France.

For Artichokes with hollandaise sauce see page 50, and Cauliflower soufflé see page 51.

Artichokes with hollandaise sauce

Artichokes

8 artichokes
3–4 litres chicken stock
2 lemons, halved

Hollandaise sauce

250g unsalted butter
15ml (1T) cold water
45ml (3T) fresh lemon juice
3ml (½t) rice vinegar (*see* Cook's notes)
7 egg yolks
pinch of white pepper
pinch of black pepper
pinch of flaked sea salt
15ml (1T) dried kooigoed leaves, chopped (*see* Cook's notes)

Artichokes

1. Wash the artichokes under cold water. Cut off the stems close to the base, pull off the tough lower petals, and trim the thorny tips of the petals using scissors.
2. In a large pot, heat the stock and add the lemon halves. When the stock comes to the boil, add the artichokes, bottoms up.
3. Cover and simmer for about 30 minutes. The artichokes are done when a knife can be inserted into the base without any resistance. Drain and keep warm until required.

Hollandaise sauce

1. Melt the butter in a small saucepan, and set aside, keeping warm.
2. Fill the bottom of a double boiler with hot water, making sure it does not touch the top bowl.
3. Put the cold water, lemon juice and rice vinegar in the top of the double boiler and whisk for a minute, using a balloon whisk.
4. Add the egg yolks, one by one, making sure each yolk is properly whisked in before adding the next one.
5. Once all the egg yolks have been mixed in, add the melted butter, a little at a time, whisking continuously.
6. Season to taste with salt and pepper and add the chopped kooigoed leaves. Pour into a jug or small bowl for serving and keep warm until required (*see* Cook's notes).

COOK'S NOTES

- You need enough chicken stock to cover the artichokes.
- To eat an artichoke, pull off a petal, dip the base in hollandaise sauce and scrape the flesh off the tender end with your front teeth. When you reach the center core of prickly leaves (the 'choke') remove it and scrape away the thistle-like fuzz to reveal the heart, the most delicious part of the artichoke.
- When making hollandaise sauce, if you don't have a double boiler, put a small metal bowl on top of a saucepan of hot water, making sure the bottom of the bowl does not touch the water. Don't allow the water in the bottom of the double boiler to boil, as this will cause the egg yolks to cook too quickly and, as a result, the sauce will curdle.
- Add the melted butter very slowly. Adding it all at once, or too quickly, will cause the sauce to curdle and separate.
- Rice vinegar, which has a slightly sweet flavour, is best for this sauce.
- Kooigoed (*Helichrysum petiolare*) is an indigenous shrub whose leaves impart a mild curry-like flavour. Instead of kooigoed, you can substitute 1T fresh lemon thyme leaves.
- It is best to serve hollandaise sauce immediately, but it can stand for up to an hour (no more). The sauce will thicken on standing. To return it to the original consistency, reheat it in the double boiler, while whisking in about 15ml (1T) of cold water.
- Use the leftover egg whites to make meringues, a soufflé or an egg-white omelette.

Cauliflower soufflé

160g (2½ cups) cauliflower florets
35ml (2½T) butter
35ml (2½T) finely chopped onion
40g (⅓ cup) cake flour, sifted
200ml (¾ cup) milk
3 eggs
35g (⅓ cup) finely grated Klein
 River Mature Gruyére Cheese
5 grinds black pepper
pinch of salt
sprigs of lemon thyme, for garnish

1. Boil the cauliflower in salted water for 10 minutes or until tender. Drain well.
2. Purée the cauliflower and set aside until needed.
3. Melt the butter in a saucepan and fry the chopped onion until soft and translucent. Do not allow it to brown.
4. Add the flour, and stir for at least 1 minute, until a firm ball forms. Turn the heat to low.
5. Using a wire whisk, slowly add the milk, ensuring that each addition is properly incorporated before adding more. Once a nice smooth sauce has been achieved, add the cheese and remove the pot from the heat.
6. Separate the eggs. Add the egg yolks, one by one, to the sauce, making sure that yolk is incorporated before you add the next one.
7. Stir in the cauliflower purée. Season with black pepper.
8. Add a pinch of salt to the egg whites. Beat to stiff points (but do not over-beat). Carefully fold the egg whites into the cauliflower mixture.
9. Pour into eight greased ramekins or silicone moulds and bake at 180°C for 30 minutes.
   Serve immediately, topped with a small sprig of lemon thyme.

COOK'S NOTES

- You can use Parmigano Reggiano instead of the mature Gruyére.
- Fold the beaten egg whites very carefully into the cauliflower cheese, as this helps to incorporate air. If you stir them in too aggressively, the soufflés will not be light enough.
- You can bake the soufflé in one dish, but increase the baking time by 10–15 minutes.

Summer fruits
in a white chocolate, almond and honey sauce

The arrival of the first white peaches and the ripening of our wild strawberries (Fragaria vesca) always heralds the start of summer for me.

White chocolate, almond and honey sauce

750ml (3 cups) fresh cream
300g white chocolate (*see* Cook's notes)
45ml (3T) Hamilton Russell Vineyards Fynbos Honey
100g flaked almonds

Fresh summer fruits

8 white peaches (*see* Cook's notes)
lemon juice, for drizzling
500ml (2 cups) raspberries
60ml (¼ cup) wild strawberries (*see* Cook's notes)
250ml (1 cup) pomegranate rubies, for garnish
fresh mint leaves, for garnish

White chocolate, almond and honey sauce

1. Heat the cream in a saucepan.
2. Break the chocolate into pieces and stir into the cream until melted.
3. Add the honey and almonds.
4. Reduce the heat to low and simmer gently for 10–15 minutes, until the sauce turns a pale caramel colour. Keep warm, or reheat gently before serving.

Fresh summer fruits

1. Slice each peach into thin wedges. Drizzle with a little lemon juice to prevent discolouration.
2. Rinse the raspberries and leave to drain, or pat dry.
3. Destalk the wild strawberries, rinse and drain, or pat dry.

To serve

Spoon some of the warm sauce into individual bowls and top with the fruit. Garnish with pomegranate rubies and sprigs of mint.

COOK'S NOTES

- You could splurge on an imported brand of chocolate, but both Cadbury's Milky Bar and Beacon Dream work very well for this recipe; just don't use cooking chocolate, the taste won't the be same.
- White peaches have light-coloured, sweet flesh and smooth, pinky-red skins that are paler in colour than nectarines. They usually arrive later in the season than nectarines and fuzzy yellow-skinned peaches.
- If you can't find wild strawberries, use roughly chopped fresh strawberries.
- You can also serve the peaches halved, filled with sauce and topped with berries, or mix the fruit and mint leaves on a platter, and serve the sauce on the side.

WINE SUGGESTIONS

You need a vibrant sweet wine to stand up to the fruit acids as well as cut through the rich, creamy sauce.
- Muscat de Frontignan Natural Sweet wine from Constantia, in the Western Cape.
- Mosel Riesling, Germany (choose a Beerenauslese or, if you prefer a richer style, a Trockenbeerenauslese).

Summer

Entertaining takes on a festive feel in December. It's holiday time and we take time off to spend with family and friends.

RIGHT Instead of store-bought ornaments, we adorn our Christmas tree with home-made biscuits, which the girls help make and decorate. FAR RIGHT Lush vine canopies, with an olive grove and pine forest in the background.

December

It's a cool December, and a little wetter than usual, which can happen so close to the sea. But this is good for the vines and their now properly formed bunches of pea-sized grapes, here and there beginning to colour a little in the Pinot Noir, as the growth of the shoots slows and the vines' energy turns to ripening. And, as the holidays approach, with the short rest prior to the final run to harvest, it is time to thin the bunches. Only the strongest shoots should bear two bunches and the weakest shoots should not have to ripen grapes. It's a costly and time-consuming exercise, but essential for quality.

Last season's Chardonnay is bottled; a good thing, as it is just in time for the festive season and the previous vintage has sold out. It is vibrant, mineral and beautiful. Tastings confirm that the Pinot Noir is ready to come out of the barrels, to be assembled to integrate and rest prior to bottling in the next month. The cellar is busy, and precision, care and cleanliness are essential. There can be no distractions.

On the clay-rich slopes of the renosterveld, so rich in species, but so visually restrained when compared to the mountain fynbos on the sandstone soils, the 'kooigoed' (*Helichrysum pandurifolium*) is in flower: small silvery, grey-green leaves mute beneath bright cream and yellow flower heads. The tiny, rust and grey-white stippled dwarf aloe (*Aloe brevifolia*) has thrown up its almost desperate flame-coloured flowers. For a month or so it's no longer so small or dull. The flowering gums are out too, in their perfectly timed, vivid Christmas reds; from burgundy to bright scarlet. On the pond below the olive grove, the floating blue-grey water lilies seem to mimic the sky reflected in the still water.

The house is full of agapanthus, hybrid tea roses and hydrangeas from the garden. The Christmas tree has been cut on the farm, installed and decorated. Entertaining takes on a festive feel, with friends and family visiting. It's holiday time, and the cool sea beckons. There's one more big wine tasting function at home and then we take some time off for family.

Gnocchi with prawn and white mussel mayonnaise
garnished with fresh avocado and almonds

This is a lovely December holiday recipe, as it is fun involving the whole family in collecting white mussels. It is best to dig for white mussels on an outgoing high tide. Press your heel into the sand to about 10 centimetres deep and feel around for the hard shell. These little creatures usually stay rather close to one another, so once you have found the first one you can expect to find more nearby.

Gnocchi
1kg (±5–6) potatoes for baking
1 egg, lightly beaten
500ml (280g) cake flour, sifted
extra flour for dusting

Prawn and white mussel mayonnaise
4 egg yolks
5ml (1t) salt
5ml (1t) mustard powder
5ml (1t) cayenne pepper
10ml (2t) Hamilton Russell
   Vineyards Fynbos Honey
45ml (3T) fresh lemon juice
125ml (½ cup) Hamilton Russell
   Vineyards Extra-virgin Olive Oil
250ml (1 cup) canola oil
45ml (3T) tomato purée
10ml (2t) Worcestershire sauce
5ml (1t) brandy
7 drops Tabasco(TM) or hot sauce
10ml (2t) fresh lemon juice
250ml (1 cup) Greek-style yoghurt
500g prawns, cooked, peeled and
   de-veined
24 white mussels, steamed and
   finely chopped (*see* Cook's notes)

To serve
4 Fuerte avocados, halved, peeled
   and stoned
fresh lemon juice, for drizzling
125ml (½ cup) lemon-infused
   olive oil
45g (8T) flaked almonds, toasted
30ml (2T) freshly grated lemon zest

Serves 8

Gnocchi
1. Preheat the oven to 180°C.
2. Scrub the potatoes, halve them and prick the skins with a fork in several places. Arrange on a roasting tray and roast for 50–70 minutes, until the skins are crispy and the insides soft. Remove from the oven, leave to cool completely, then peel off the skins and the crispy layer.
3. Mash the potatoes until smooth. Form the mashed potato into a mound and create a hollow in the middle.
4. Pour the lightly beaten egg into the hollow of the mashed potato. Sprinkle the sifted flour over the mash. Using a wooden spoon, mix the egg and flour into the mash until a firm ball forms (don't overwork the mixture or the gnocchi will become too paste-like).
5. Sprinkle a work surface with flour and flour your hands. Divide the mash into eight pieces. Gently roll each piece into a cylinder about 2.5cm thick. Cut into 3cm pieces, pressing the pieces against the tines of a fork to form an indentation.
6. As the gnocchi are made, place them on a lightly floured baking tray or in an airtight container lined with wax paper or baking paper. (They can be frozen at this point.)
7. Bring a large pot of salted water to the boil. Gently drop in the gnocchi (fresh or frozen), a few at a time. Lift them out with a slotted spoon as they rise to the surface, and drain in a colander. Repeat until all the gnocchi have been cooked. Serve immediately.

Prawn and white mussel mayonnaise
1. Put the egg yolks, salt, mustard powder, cayenne pepper, honey and 30ml (2T) lemon juice into the bowl of an electric mixer. Beat for 15 seconds.
2. Combine the two oils. With the motor running at high speed, add the oils to the egg mixture, one drop at a time (this should take 12–15 minutes). The mixture should thicken with every addition of oil. If you add the oil too quickly, it will become too thin and you'll need to start again.
3. When all the oil has been added and the mixture is thick and glossy, beat in 15ml lemon juice.
4. In a separate bowl, combine the tomato purée, Worcestershire sauce, brandy, Tabasco, lemon juice and yoghurt. Stir into the mayonnaise.
5. Add the prawns and white mussels to the mayonnaise and stir gently to combine.

To serve
Slice the avocados thinly and sprinkle with lemon juice to prevent discolouration. Divide the gnocchi between eight serving bowls. Drizzle over some lemon-infused olive oil and top with a spoonful of prawn and mussel mayonnaise and half a sliced avocado. Top with toasted almonds and a sprinkling of lemon zest.

COOK'S NOTES:
- For a speedier gnocchi, buy 1.2kg ready-made gnocchi and cook according to the instructions.
- If you have harvested your own white mussels, steam them in salted water until the shells open (discard any that don't open). Remove the meat and cut the muscular 'tongue' from the innards (it is easily visible, shaped like a shark's tooth). Use the tongue and discard the rest of the meat.
- Instead of white mussels, you can use clams, alikreukels or periwinkles.
- You need a permit (from the post office) to collect white mussels. The limit is 50 per person per day, with a minimum size of 35mm.
- To make lemon-infused olive oil, pare the skin and zest of four lemons and place in a 500ml bottle of fresh extra-virgin olive oil (discard the flesh or pips, as they will make the oil bitter). Leave for two months to infuse. Lemon-infused olive oil is available from most supermarkets.

WINE SUGGESTIONS
This flavoursome and creamy dish requires a fresh, structured dry Rosé.
- Dry Rosé from Durbanville, Western Cape.
- Domaines Ott Chateau de Selle Rosé Coeur de Grain Cru Classe, Côtes de Provence.
- Sancerre Rosé, Loire region, France.

In Summer, the cellar is busy, and precision, care and cleanliness are essential.

LEFT Agapanthus comes into flower at this time of the year.

RIGHT In the cellar, a previous vintage of Pinot Noir is moved to tanks in preparation for bottling.

LEFT The intricate, delicate flower of the passion fruit (*Passiflora edulis*).

RIGHT Empty Pinot noir barrels waiting to be washed in readiness for the coming harvest.

Roast turkey with sage and orange stuffing
with cranberry and Pinot Noir sauce and deep-fried vine leaves

At Christmas, we love indulging in a traditional turkey with all the trimmings. I give it my own twist by adding crispy, deep-fried vine leaves and an aromatic cranberry sauce made with our own Pinot Noir.

Brining the turkey

3–4kg turkey, thawed (*see* Cook's notes, page 66)
water
salt (½ cup per 4 litres of water)
white sugar (¼ cup per 4 litres of water)
1 orange, sliced into wedges
1 sprig fresh rosemary
2 dried bay leaves
2ml (¼t) coriander seeds

Roasting the turkey

65g (5T) butter
water
one orange, cut into wedges

Sage and orange stuffing

7 slices white bread
75g (6T) butter
30ml (2T) Hamilton Russell Vineyards
   Extra-virgin Olive Oil
1 medium onion, finely chopped
2–3 cloves freshly chopped garlic
40g celery, finely chopped
300g salciccia sausage meat (*see* Cook's
   notes, page 66)
25g fresh sage leaves, chopped
15ml (1T) chopped flat-leaf parsley
15ml (1T) grated orange zest
60ml (¼ cup) fresh orange juice
freshly ground black pepper

Serves 8

Brining the turkey

1. Start preparing this dish the day before. You will need a bowl or basin with a lid, big enough to hold the turkey, but also able to fit into the fridge. (*See* Cook's notes, page 66.)
2. Make up a brine solution using ½ cup salt and ¼ cup sugar for every 4 litres of cold water. Place the thawed turkey into the brine, making sure it is completely submerged.
3. Add the orange wedges to the brine, along with the herbs and spices.
4. Put into the fridge and leave for 6–8 hours (about 1 hour per 500g).
5. Remove the turkey from the brine, rinse well, pat dry, place in a shallow dish, cover and leave in the fridge for at least 1 hour (preferably overnight), to help the skin crisp.

Roasting the turkey

1. Preheat the oven to 180°C.
2. Rub one tablespoon of butter into the cavity of the bird.
3. Carefully loosen the skin from the breasts and thighs, ensuring the skin does not tear.
4. Rub one tablespoon of butter under the skin of each breast.
5. Place some stuffing under the breast and thigh skin, and the rest in the cavity.
6. Truss the turkey and place it on a rack in a roasting tray, breast-side up. Add cold water to below the level of the rack.
7. Rub one tablespoon of butter over the top of the bird.
8. Place the orange wedges on the rack around the bird.
9. Cover with a lid or heavy aluminium foil (shiny side in) and roast for 90 minutes.
10. Remove the lid or foil, melt the last tablespoon of butter and brush over the breasts. Roast for another 60–90 minutes (total cooking time should be about 45 minutes per kg). To test for doneness, pierce the thickest part of the thigh with a skewer or sharp knife. If the juices run clear, the turkey is done. If you need to continue cooking the turkey for more than an hour, cover the breast and thighs and the tips of the wings and drumsticks with foil to ensure they don't brown too much or dry out.
11. Remove the turkey from the oven and set aside, loosely covered with foil, to rest for 20–30 minutes before carving.

Sage and orange stuffing

1. Preheat the oven to 90°C. Gently toast the bread until the slices turn light golden brown and start to harden slightly, 3–5 minutes depending on how fresh the bread is.
2. Crumb the toasted bread in a food processor. Set aside.
3. Melt the butter in a large pan, add the olive oil, onion, garlic and celery, and fry over medium heat until the onion becomes translucent and the celery starts to soften slightly.
4. Add the crumbs and the rest of the ingredients, and fry until the sausage meat is cooked, about 5–7 minutes. Remove from the heat and set aside to cool completely.

For Cranberry and Pinot Noir sauce and Deep-fried vine leaves, see page 66.

Cranberry and Pinot Noir sauce

1 tin (400g) jellied cranberry sauce
160ml (⅔ cup) Hamilton Russell
    Vineyards Pinot Noir
45ml (3T) dark soy sauce
50g dried cranberries

Deep-fried vine leaves

250ml (1 cup) Hamilton Russell
    Vineyards Extra-virgin Olive Oil
16 fresh vine leaves, rinsed and
    dried well (*see* Cook's notes)

Fresh vine leaves, for garnish

Cranberry and Pinot Noir sauce

1. Place all the ingredients in a saucepan and heat over medium heat, stirring, until the jelly melts.
2. Reduce the heat and simmer for 5 minutes (do not allow it to boil). Pour into a jug and keep warm until required.

Deep-fried vine leaves

1. Heat the oil in a medium saucepan and fry the vine leaves, in batches, for a few seconds until crispy. Drain on a paper towel.

To serve

Place the turkey on a platter surrounded by deep-fried vine leaves. Garnish the dish with fresh vine leaves. Serve the sauce separately on the side.

COOK'S NOTES

- Ensure the turkey is completely thawed before brining. A 3–4kg bird takes ± 42 hours to thaw in the fridge.
- Do not brine a self-basting turkey; this will already have a salty stock added and brining will make it too salty.
- When brining the turkey, a handy space-saving solution is to thoroughly wash and rinse one of your fridge's vegetable drawers. Place the turkey and brine in the largest cooking or freezer bag you can find, seal the bag and place it in the vegetable drawer. Alternatively, place the turkey, in cooking a bag, inside a large, rigid cooler box, and pack additional bags of ice around the bird to keep it cool. (Don't use a bin liner or garbage bag to hold the turkey, as they are not made from 'food grade' plastic.)
- Salciccia are Tuscan-style pork sausages, made in the traditional way, and flavoured with black pepper, garlic, coriander and cayenne pepper. You can use 3–4 good-quality pork sausages instead. Remove the meat from the casings and mix gently with a fork before adding to the other stuffing ingredients.
- If you don't have a food processor, crumb the toasted bread by placing the slices on a dry work surface, cover with a clean tea towel and crush with a rolling pin.
- It is best to make the stuffing a day ahead and store it in the fridge overnight, as it must be completely cool before being placed in the turkey.
- Pick young and tender vine leaves which have not been sprayed with any pesticides. Ensure the leaves are completely dry before frying them in the oil.

WINE SUGGESTIONS

A Christmas classic, requiring a terroir-driven, rich and generous red wine that is starting to show its mature side.
- Pinot Noir from Hemel-en-Aarde Valley, with at least 7 years of age.
- Pinot Noir from Oregon, USA (at least 5 years old).
- For a really special occasion, Gevrey-Chambertin Grand Cru, one of the great Burgundies.

Roasted sweet potato chips with chilli and ginger

1.2kg sweet potatoes
60ml (¼ cup) Hamilton Russell
    Vineyards Extra-virgin Olive Oil
15ml (1T) butter
30ml (2T) Hamilton Russell
    Vineyards Chardonnay
30ml (2T) freshly chopped ginger
2ml (¼t) dried chilli, chopped

1. Scrub the sweet potatoes, but do not peel. Cut into chips.
2. Bring a pot of salted water to the boil. Boil the chips for 5 minutes, then drain and pat dry.
3. Preheat the oven to 180°C. Heat the olive oil, butter and wine in a roasting tray.
4. Spread the sweet potato chips in the roasting tray and sprinkle with ginger and chilli. Shake the pan to coat the potatoes in the buttery olive oil.
5. Roast for 50–60 minutes, turning the potatoes every 15–20 minutes.

Ginger biscuit ice cream
with cranberry and orange jelly

All the Christmas flavours combined in one cool summer pudding!

Ginger biscuit mix

50g (4T) butter
60ml (¼ cup) brown sugar
60ml (¼ cup) golden syrup
1 egg
300ml (1¼ cups) cake flour, sifted
10ml (½T) ground ginger
2ml (¼t) mixed spice
2ml (¼t) bicarbonate of soda

Ginger biscuit ice cream

500ml (2 cups) fresh cream
2ml (¼t) ground ginger
60ml (¼ cup) castor sugar
4 egg yolks
3ml (½t) vanilla paste

Cranberry and orange jelly

500ml (2 cups) clear apple juice
50g gelatine powder
500ml (2 cups) cranberry juice
500ml (2 cups) orange juice
500ml (2 cups) pomegranate juice
100g dried cranberries

granadilla pulp, for garnish
fresh mint leaves, for garnish

Serves 8

Ginger biscuit mix

1. Using an electric beater, cream the butter and sugar until pale and creamy.
2. Add the golden syrup and egg while still beating.
3. Stir in the dry ingredients until the mixture comes together.
4. Knead and shape into a ball. Wrap in cling wrap and refrigerate for 30 minutes.
5. Preheat the oven to 180°C. Roll out the biscuit mix to 5mm thick. Bake on a greased tray for about 10 minutes until light brown. Turn onto a rack and leave to cool, then crush into a coarse crumble.

Ginger biscuit ice cream

1. Heat the cream in a pot, add the ground ginger, and remove just before boiling.
2. In an electric mixer, whisk the sugar, egg yolks and vanilla paste until thick and pale yellow (± 5 minutes).
3. Pour the warm cream into the egg mixture while whisking slowly for about 2 minutes.
4. Return the mixture to the pot and heat slowly while stirring continuously. Remove from the heat once the mixture coats the back of a spoon, but before it begins to boil.
5. Transfer to a metal bowl and immerse in an ice bath to stop it cooking any further. Stir occasionally until it has cooled (about 15 minutes), then stir in half the ginger biscuit crumbs.
6. Transfer to an ice cream machine and churn. Add the remaining biscuit crumbs before the ice cream freezes.

Cranberry and orange jelly

1. Spray a 2 litre-capacity ring-mould with non-stick cooking spray.
2. Pour the apple juice into a medium saucepan and heat gently. When it comes to the boil, reduce the heat to a simmer. Sprinkle 25g gelatine into the hot, but not boiling, juice and stir to dissolve.
3. Remove from the heat and add the cranberry juice, stirring to combine. Pour the apple-cranberry juice into the mould and leave to cool, then refrigerate for 3 hours, or until firm.
4. While the first layer is setting, pour the orange juice, pomegranate juice and dried cranberries into a pot and heat gently. Once boiling, remove from the heat and set aside for 30 minutes for the cranberries to plump.
5. Place about a quarter of the juice (without cranberries) in a small saucepan. Bring back to the boil, then reduce the heat to a simmer and dissolve the rest of the gelatine powder in the juice. Remove from the heat and stir into the orange-pomegranate juice. Set aside for 10–20 minutes to cool.
6. Remove the mould from the fridge and carefully pour the orange and pomegranate juice over the apple-cranberry jelly. Put back into the fridge for another 4–5 hours until set.

To serve

Take the ice cream out of the freezer 30 minutes before serving to soften slightly. Unmould the jelly and scoop the ice cream into the centre of the jelly. Top with granadilla pulp and fresh mint leaves and serve immediately.

COOK'S NOTES

- You can make the jelly a day or two in advance. Once set, cover with a lid or cling wrap.
- A silicone ring-mould works best, as it does not leak and it is easy to unmould the jelly.
- Try to find 100% cranberry juice, like Ocean Spray. If you use a cranberry-apple blend, omit the apple juice and use one litre of blended juice.

WINE SUGGESTIONS

Ginger adds personality to this delicate dessert, so a wine of precision and freshness will be perfect.

- Rosé Methode Cap Classique from Stellenbosch, Western Cape.
- Champagne Grand Cru Blanc de Noir from Bouzy, France.

ABOVE Looking down on Hermanus from the ridge on the Estate.

RIGHT The kelp beds of Walker Bay are home to Cape rock lobster, locally known as crayfish.

FAR RIGHT Fragrant star jasmine fills the air with the scent of summer.

January

A new calendar year has begun, but the old season is merely approaching closure. It is warm now, with nature fading slightly in the drier heat of midsummer. It's been the driest January in years, but there is still plenty of water in the dams. The shrill ring of cicadas is a regular, somehow deeply comforting, sound. At night in the still, cool air, small frogs replace the cicadas with their own raucous chorus. The gentle southeasterly breeze brings in the deep, damp smell of the sea just over the ridge behind the house.

The vineyard team is back after the holidays and hard at work in the vineyards. Shoot positioning is finessed in the trellising wires and the occasional bunches that have not coloured with the majority are removed. We don't want to risk picking less ripe grapes, as this reduces flavour concentration. Narrow, protective bird nets are installed over the bunch zone in the sensitive areas of the vineyards, on the borders and near protective vegetation. More raptor posts are installed to give the patrolling birds of prey, steppe buzzards in particular, an easy perch and lookout point. They keep the grape eaters on the wing.

In the cellar, last year's Pinot Noir is bottled. It is vibrant, bright and perfumed, with its characteristic ancient, almost primal, savoury notes. With both wines in the bottle, the cellar risk has been greatly reduced, just as the vineyard risk escalates. New small oak barrels for the coming harvest arrive from France and are washed, prepared and neatly stacked. The cellar is ready for harvest.

On the stony ridge in the nature reserve overlooking the bay, the vygie (*Lampranthus furvus*) is in flower. The small neat bushes, with their bright pink, yellow-centred flowers, look like sugar-iced loaves. There are a lot of players out on the fynbos stage, but for many their debut was a while back. They are tired and look it. But the hybrid tea roses in the stone-walled garden aren't tired and there is something bright and perfumed to pick for the house every day. The forest sugar gums are in full flower and the trees are alive with bees. In a couple of weeks the first of the new eucalypt honey will be harvested; light, liquid and fragrant.

Friends have stayed on for a while after Christmas in the Cape, and many from overseas have chosen this beautiful month to holiday here and tour the vineyards. It is a peak time for visitors: casual consumers and professionals alike.

Chilled cucumber and wild sorrel soup
garnished with white milkwood berry syrup

White milkwood (*Sideroxylon inerme*) is one of South Africa's protected trees. It grows mainly in the coastal areas. The berries ripen in summer and have succulent purple flesh with sticky white juice. Sorrel (*Rumex acetosa*) is a garden herb, but it also grows wild in grasslands with acidic soils. It has a lovely sharp lemony flavour.

Chilled cucumber soup

1½ litres (6 cups) vegetable stock
2 English cucumbers (± 700g), peeled, cored and diced
1 celery stalk (± 50g), sliced
1 fennel bulb (± 90g), sliced
2 shallots or small onions, chopped
30ml (2T) cornflour
250ml (1 cup) plain fat-free yoghurt
15ml (1T) fresh lemon juice
½ cup fresh, shredded sorrel leaves (*see* Cook's notes)
salt and pepper, to taste

Garnish

8 ripe milkwood berries (*see* Cook's notes)
45ml (3T) Greek-style yoghurt
10ml (2t) caviar (*see* Cook's notes)

Serves 8

Chilled cucumber soup

1. In a medium saucepan, bring the stock to the boil.
2. Add the cucumbers, celery, fennel and shallots and simmer until soft, about 20 minutes.
3. Set aside to cool slightly, then blend or liquidize.
4. Return to a clean pot and reheat until just simmering.
5. Mix the cornflour with a little water to form a smooth paste, and add to the pot.
6. Stir in the yoghurt, and cook until the mixture thickens slightly (*see* Cook's notes).
7. Remove from the heat and add the sorrel leaves and lemon juice. Season to taste with salt and pepper.
8. Leave to cool slightly and chill in the fridge for at least 2 hours before serving.
9. To squeeze the syrup from the milkwood berries, make a small cut in each berry, then roll it between two teaspoons to extract the juice. Set the juice aside, discarding the flesh.

To serve

Serve the soup in wine glasses or small bowls. Top each one with a teaspoon of Greek yoghurt and a dab of caviar, and drizzle with milkwood berry syrup. This is delicious when accompanied by warm focaccia flavoured with pine nuts and flaked sea salt (*see* page 14).

COOK'S NOTES

*   You can use either garden sorrel or wild sorrel. Use slightly less garden sorrel, as it has a more intense flavour. Remove the spines from the sorrel leaves before shredding.
*   The soup can come to the boil after the yoghurt is added, but do not let it boil once the sorrel and lemon juice have been added, or it will curdle.
*   Use the syrup from just one milkwood berry per serving, as the milky juice has a rather strong flavour and a slightly bitter aftertaste. When the berries are ripe, the skin turns a dark purple-black and the pulp softens slightly. When squeezed, the sticky, milky syrup will appear.
*   Instead of real caviar, you can use red or black lumpfish caviar or seaweed caviar.

WINE SUGGESTIONS

The refreshing elements in this soup will be a perfect match for a clean, light and crisp minerally white.
*   Single vineyard, limestone-grown, unoaked Chardonnay from Robertson in the Western Cape.
*   Petit Chablis from a reputable French producer.
*   Verdicchio di Matelica *or* Verdicchio dei Castelli di Jesi from Italy's Adriatic coast (look for the term 'Classico Superiore' on the label).

Our Frantoio olive trees were planted in 1996, although olive oil was first made on Hamilton Russell Vineyards in 1993.

LEFT The olive grove surrounding the house.

RIGHT The still-forming fruits of the prickly pear cactus (*Opuntia ficus-indica*).

LEFT Hybrid tea roses provide cut flowers for the house.

RIGHT At this time of year, the Frantoio olives are still a couple of months away from harvest.

Walker Bay crayfish
with lemon, ginger and coriander sauce

The heady scent of pink-tinged Jasminum officinale flowers on a balmy summer evening always evokes memories of happy and relaxed holidays. Summer at the Cape is a time to enjoy freshly caught crayfish (rock lobster). We love to invite friends to the farm in early January to celebrate the start of another year over a long lunch. Depending on the size of the crayfish, allow one to two per person.

Crayfish

16 Walker Bay crayfish, cleaned
  and prepared
15 litres sea water or salted water

Jasmine-scented basmati rice

1½ litres (6 cups) salted water
¼ cup fresh *Jasminum officinale*
  flowers (these are edible)
30ml (2T) rice vinegar
500ml (2 cups) basmati rice
15ml (1T) white sugar

Lemon, ginger and coriander sauce

60ml (4T) fresh ginger, peeled
  and grated
15ml (1T) freshly grated lemon rind
15ml (1T) freshly chopped garlic
10ml (2t) Hamilton Russell
  Vineyards Fynbos Honey
80ml (⅓ cup) fresh lemon juice
45ml (3T) dark soy sauce
45ml (3T) teriyaki sauce
500ml (2 cups) Hamilton Russell
  Vineyards Extra-virgin Olive Oil
250ml (1 cup) fresh coriander,
  chopped

fresh coriander to garnish
fresh jasmine flowers to garnish

Serves 8

Crayfish

1. In a pot (or two) large enough to hold all the crayfish, bring the sea water to the boil. (For fresh water, add 35ml (2½T) salt per litre.)
2. Add the crayfish and bring back to the boil. When the water starts bubbling, set the timer for 7 minutes. Turn the heat off after 7 minutes, but leave the crayfish in the pot, with the lid on, for a further 3 minutes, then drain.
3. Remove the tails by twisting and slowly pulling them off the bodies. Rinse the body cavities under fresh, running water, and set aside. (Leave the legs and feelers attached to the bodies.)
4. Rinse the tails and use kitchen scissors to cut each one lengthways through the underside (soft part) of the carapace, then use a sharp knife to carefully slit the flesh so that you can take out the alimentary tract. Set the tails aside.
5. To reheat the crayfish before serving, dunk them in boiling water for a minute and drain briefly.

Jasmine-scented basmati rice

1. Rinse the rice under cold water. Drain well.
2. Bring the salted water to the boil, add the jasmine flowers and 15ml (1T) of rice vinegar.
3. After 2 minutes, add the rice and cook, uncovered, for 12 minutes. Stir occasionally to prevent the rice from sticking to the bottom of the pot; lower the heat if necessary.
4. Remove from the heat, add the other tablespoon of the rice vinegar and the tablespoon of sugar. Mix to combine and leave to stand, uncovered, for 20 minutes. Reheat before serving. (If you don't have fresh jasmine flowers, you can use jasmine-scented rice.)

Lemon, ginger and coriander sauce

1. Combine all the ingredients, except the olive oil and coriander, in a blender or liquidizer and blend for 2 minutes.
2. While the blender is running, add the olive oil in a slow stream. Once all the oil has been added, blend for another minute.
3. Add the fresh coriander and pulse for three seconds. Pour the sauce into a pot and reheat gently; do not allow to boil. (If you make the sauce in advance, it may separate on reheating; simply whisk gently with a wire whisk.)

To serve

Arrange the crayfish bodies on a large platter, tails towards the center. Pour a bit of warm sauce onto each tail and sprinkle with fresh coriander. Serve the remaining sauce on the side. Spoon the rice into a serving bowl. Garnish with fresh herbs and flowers.

COOK'S NOTES

- To kill live crayfish humanely, put them into the freezer for a few hours, until they are frozen, then plunge them into fresh water. This will kill them.
- Thaw frozen crayfish by placing them in water for 30–60 minutes. Periodically feel inside the tail to determine whether the flesh has thawed.
- To cook the crayfish in batches, scoop them out after 3 minutes standing time, bring the water back to the boil and repeat with the next batch of crayfish. It is not necessary to start with a fresh pot of salted water every time.
- Crayfish (rock lobster) may only be caught at certain times of the year and a permit (available from any post office) is required. Catches are subject to a daily limit and strict size restrictions. Commercially caught crayfish are available from seafood retailers.
- Cape rock lobster (*Jasus lalandii*) known locally as crayfish or 'kreef', comes from a different family to the freshwater crayfish (crawfish or écrevisses) of North America and Europe, and is not closely related to clawed (Maine) lobsters.

WINE SUGGESTIONS

For this Asian-influenced crayfish, choose a subtly wooded, minerally white wine with citrus notes, or try a wine with a floral, stone-fruit character and a delicately creamy texture.
- Chardonnay from Hemel-en-Aarde Valley (3 years old) with vibrant citrus fruit.
- New wave Grenache Blanc from Paarl, Western Cape.
- Dry Gewürztraminer from Alsace, France.

Honey panna cotta
with Chardonnay-poached prickly pears and fresh prickly pears

The prickly pear (Opuntia ficus-indica), also known as an Indian fig opuntia, is a species of paddle cactus introduced to South Africa from Central America in the 19th century. The flesh of the fruits is bright red-purple or yellow-white and contains many tiny, hard seeds that are usually swallowed, but should be avoided if you have a problem digesting seeds. Jams and jellies produced from the fruit resemble strawberries or figs in colour and flavour. If prickly pears are not available, you can substitute firm, ripe, fresh pears.

Honey panna cotta

500ml (2 cups) fresh cream
300ml (1¼ cups) full-cream milk
4 rooibos teabags
60ml (4T) Hamilton Russell
   Vineyards Fynbos Honey
3ml (½t) vanilla paste
5 sheets gelatine

Poached prickly pears

750ml (3 cups) Hamilton Russell
   Vineyards Chardonnay
45ml (3T) Hamilton Russell
   Vineyards Fynbos Honey
4 prickly pears, peeled and halved
1 rooibos teabag

4 fresh prickly pears, peeled and
   quartered, for serving

Serves 8

Honey panna cotta

1. Combine all the ingredients, except the gelatine, in a large pot. Bring to the boil, then remove from the heat and leave, covered, for 1 hour for the flavours to infuse.
2. Soak the gelatine sheets in cold water for 5 minutes. Squeeze out all the water before using.
3. Spray 8 panna cotta moulds or ramekins (125ml capacity) with non-stick cooking spray.
4. Reheat the cream. As soon as it starts to boil, remove from the heat. Remove the tea bags and add the gelatine sheets, stirring gently until they dissolve.
5. Pour the hot cream into the moulds, set aside to cool and then refrigerate for at least 3 hours, until set. The panna cotta can be made up to two days in advance. Keep cold until ready to serve.

Chardonnay-poached prickly pears

1. Place the wine and honey in a medium saucepan and heat gently until the honey is melted and the liquid comes to the boil.
2. Add the prickly pear halves and the rooibos teabag. Turn down the heat and simmer for 10 minutes, removing the teabag after 5 minutes.
3. Remove the prickly pears with a slotted spoon and set aside.
4. Turn the heat back up and reduce the poaching liquid by half (this should take 3–5 minutes). Decant into a jug and set aside (in the fridge or at room temperature) until needed.

To serve

Unmould each panna cotta into an individual bowl. Garnish with a poached prickly pear half and two quarters of fresh prickly pear and drizzle with the reduced poaching liquid.

COOK'S NOTES

- To set the panna cotta, use five sheets of gelatine (±11 x 8cm each). Gelatine sheets are best but if you use powdered gelatine, dissolve 20g (6½t) in 150ml of hot liquid and add to the mixture.
- Wear protective gloves when picking and handling prickly pears. Fresh prickly pears are typically eaten after being chilled for a few hours; I find it easiest to use a knife and fork to peel them.
- The spineless sweet prickly pear (*Opuntia ficus-indica*) is grown commercially. The flesh, which contains many small seeds, can be bright red/purple or white/yellowish. Prickly pears are best eaten when chilled.

WINE SUGGESTIONS

This dessert is full of flavour. To liven it up, try a slightly mature sparkling wine. A vintage Blanc de Blancs from France's Champagne region would be the perfect ending to a special meal.
- Vintage Méthode Cap Classique Blanc des Blancs (100% Chardonnay) from Robertson, Western Cape.
- Champagne Blanc de Blancs from Le Mesnil Grand Cru vineyards, France.

February is the month of the harvest; Nature's finale. This is what the year's vineyard work has built towards.

RIGHT Between them, Saul and Makhadi handle several tons of grapes each harvest day.
FAR RIGHT Ricardo passes crates of hand-harvested Pinot Noir grapes to the crusher team.

February

This is the month of the harvest; Nature's finale and what all the year's vineyard work has built towards. The numerous subtle influences of site, soil, rain, sun and wind are all there in the grapes, ready to be expressed as wine. A thing of beauty. The story of place at a point in time. It is a time of year when priorities are clear. The grapes must come in at exactly the right moment: too early or too late, and something is lost. And, like clockwork, the earliest of the Pinot Noir is ripe to readiness in the first week of February. Our initial hand has been dealt and it is now the cellar team's job to play it well, respecting both the unchanging character of site and the particular personality of the year. It can take 50 days from the first grapes to the last. We will gamble with nature for a while yet.

Our cellar team has swollen to include experienced young winemaking assistants from Burgundy and the Loire, California and, this year, Argentina. Wine is in their blood and their families' blood, and all have worked in cellars around the world. They are here to learn and to exchange ideas, and don't mind the long nights and early mornings. To everyone, the wine comes first. The world of fine wine is a small one, with a common language. The cellar is a hive of activity.

Although it is sometimes known as a March lily, February is our time for the belladonna lily (*Amaryllis belladonna*). Coloured a fine, fresh, baby pink, its scent is almost indescribably beautiful; a rare soap on an ancient Mediterranean beauty, warm and intoxicating, but cool and clean as well. On the mountain fynbos slopes behind the house, the brilliant scarlet everlastings (*Phaenocoma prolifera*) have flushed with new growth; a hot blush on the cheeks of the hills. In the late evening, bats, like drunk, youthful aviators, conduct their jagged fly-pasts of the garden lights, seeking moths. The warm nights are noisy too. Now the repetitive ring of the crickets joins the deeper rasp of the frogs. It's their month.

The clean warmth, even heat, of February, our hottest month, draws those escaping the cold of Europe and North America. We receive record numbers of wine-loving visitors. They relish the weather as well as the drama of harvest and we are grateful for their interest and proud to show them our wines. What we do and why we do it is something that is particularly clear in February.

Ravioli of alikreukel and seaweed
in a chilli, lemongrass and coconut milk broth

Alikreukel, also known as giant periwinkle or 'ollicrock', is most often dived out, but it can sometimes be found in rock pools at low tide in the less-populated parts of the Cape Coast. 'Nori seaweed', which can be plucked from the rocks at low tide, is believed to have the most protein of all the seaweed varieties, and is also rich in calcium and iodine.

Chilli, lemongrass and coconut milk broth

800ml (3 cups) coconut milk
2cm piece of lemongrass, finely
  chopped
10ml (2t) sesame oil
10ml (2t) dark soy sauce
5ml (1t) green curry paste
4 slices pickled jalapeño chillies,
  very finely chopped

Alikreukel and seaweed filling

3 alikreukels in the shell
  (± 60g meat in total)
30ml (2T) fresh nori seaweed or
  1½ sheets dried nori seaweed
  (*see* Cook's notes)

Ravioli dough

300g cake flour, sifted
100g semolina, sifted
4 eggs
olive oil, for cooking
salt, for cooking

black seaweed caviar, for garnish
  (*see* Cook's notes)
sprigs or fresh coriander leaves or
  flowers, for garnish

Serves 8

Chilli, lemongrass and coconut milk broth

1. Place all the ingredients in a medium saucepan and heat slowly.
2. Remove from the heat when it starts to boil.
3. Set aside, covered, for at least 30 minutes to allow the flavours to infuse.
4. Reheat gently before serving.

Alikreukel and seaweed filling

1. Wash the alikreukels to remove any sand. Bring a pot of lightly salted water to the boil and cook the alikreukels, in their shells, for about 20 minutes, until the meat loosens and starts pushing out of the shell.
2. Remove the alikreukels from the pot and cut off the firm white meat, discarding the rest. Chop the white meat finely and set aside.
3. Rinse the fresh seaweed well under cold running water to remove all traces of sand. Chop very finely. If you are using dried nori seaweed, crumble the sheets.
4. Combine the chopped seaweed and alikreukel meat and place in the fridge until needed.

Making the ravioli dough

1. Place the cake flour, semolina and eggs in the bowl of an electric mixer.
2. Using the dough hook, mix on medium speed until a homogenous mix has been achieved. Continue mixing until the dough becomes smooth and forms a firm ball. It should not be sticky; if it is, add a little extra semolina. (If you can't knead the dough into a firm ball in the mixer, tip it onto a floured work surface and knead by hand.)
3. When the dough stops sticking to the bowl or the work surface, shape it into three or four fist-sized balls, wrapping each one tightly in cling wrap.
4. Leave at room temperature for 30 minutes, to allow the gluten to relax. (Don't leave it for much longer than 30 minutes.)

Rolling the dough and shaping the ravioli

1. Adjust a pasta-rolling machine to setting 7. Take one ball of dough and run it through twice (this might be tricky, but just flatten the dough slightly and push it through). Although the dough will break up, this initial rolling 'forces' the ingredients together.
2. Fold the pieces together. If the dough is slightly sticky, add a touch more flour; if the dough is too dry or starts to crack, wet your hands while working with it.
3. Set the pasta machine to setting 2 and run the dough through twice. Adjust the setting to 3 and run it through twice again. By now the strip of dough should have lengthened quite a bit. If you join the ends by overlapping them by about 3cm, you can run the dough through the machine in a continuous loop, which allows you to work a bit faster.
4. Continue running the dough though twice on each setting, up to number 7.
5. Cut the strip of dough into a single length, and lay it on a floured surface. Cover with a dry tea towel, topped with a damp tea towel (this will prevent the strip form drying out too much until you are ready to cut it). If there are two of you, one person can start cutting the sheets while the other gets on with the rolling process.
6. Repeat with the rest of the dough balls.
7. Once all the dough has been rolled and the strips laid out, cut out heart shapes using a cookie cutter measuring ±7cm across.
8. Start filling and sealing the ravioli immediately, as it will become increasingly difficult to seal the parcels properly if the dough dries out too much. Allow three to five ravioli per person.

Assembling and cooking the ravioli

1. Place half a teaspoon of filling on half of the ravioli cut-outs.
2. To seal the ravioli pockets, dip your finger in water and run it around the edge of the shape. Place another ravioli cut-out on top (floured side to the outside) and crimp the edges between your thumb and forefinger, moving around the edge until the parcel is sealed. (At this point, the ravioli parcels can be layered between sheets of wax paper and stored in the freezer, in an airtight container, for up to one week, until needed.)
3. Bring a large pot of water to the boil. Add a pinch of salt and a dollop of olive oil, then add the ravioli slowly, keeping the water on the boil.
4. Fresh pasta cooks very quickly, so the ravioli should only need about 3 minutes. They will float to the top when ready. Carefully spoon the ravioli into a colander (set over a bowl) and set aside briefly to drain. If you can't fit all the ravioli into the pot at once, cook them in batches. Frozen ravioli don't need to be defrosted before cooking.

To serve

Arrange the ravioli pockets on a plate and spoon over some warm broth. Garnish with black seaweed caviar, a grinding of black pepper and a few sprigs of coriander. Serve immediately.

WINE SUGGESTIONS

This briny, sea-influenced ravioli needs a tangy and structured white wine to support the broth.

*   South African fino-style sherry, chilled.
*   Manzanilla, a delicate, fino-style sherry from Sanlúcar de Barrameda in Andalusia, Spain.
*   Muscadet-Sèvre et Maine *sur lie*, Loire, France.
*   White Vinho Verde from northern Portugal, or Albariño from Galicia, Spain.

COOK'S NOTES

*   'Nori' is the Japanese name for an edible seaweed of the *Porphyra* genus (known as 'laver' in England). Nori is widely available in dried form; you'll need 1½ sheets for this recipe (use ready-to-use sushi nori, not the type that has to be toasted first). If you live at the coast, you can collect fresh seaweed off the rocks. Two pieces should yield about 30ml (2T) shredded seaweed. Store fresh seaweed in seawater until needed and rinse well before use. You can substitute 30ml (2T) of mixed fresh rocket, coriander and basil leaves, finely chopped.
*   Fresh alikreukel freezes very well in the shell. Before using, thaw at room temperature and then boil for about 40 minutes.
*   Instead of alikreukel, you can use calamari steaks. Poach one small steak until the meat turns opaque (take care not to over-cook). Cool completely, then chop finely.
*   To make the pasta dough by hand: place the flour and semolina in a mound on a clean, flat work surface. Make a well in centre and crack in the eggs, then use a fork to slowly mix the eggs into the flour. Once the egg and flour mixture is combined, start kneading, and follow the method on page 86.
*   Seaweed caviar comes in red, black and 'wasabi green' versions (*see also* page 31).

Acheulean hand axes and rubbing stones dating from the Late Stone Age have been found on Hamilton Russell Vineyards, evidence of this area's long, unbroken history of human occupation.

LEFT Magda heads up a line of vineyard workers picking Pinot Noir grapes.

RIGHT A granite cross stands sentinal on a hillock in the fynbos.

LEFT A bunch of Chardonnay grapes is harvested at perfect ripeness.

RIGHT This cross, carved into the sandstone ridge high above the bay, dates from the 15th century, when Portuguese explorers first rounded the Cape of Good Hope.

Kingklip with a parsley crème fraîche sauce
with beetroot and cardamom pap with edamame beans

Kingklip is a fish with a lovely mild flavour and firm, large-flaked flesh. The tapered body allows for long, relatively bone-free fillets. February is the month of love so, for a special Valentine's Day meal, I use beetroot juice to add a touch of pink and heart-shaped moulds for the accompanying pap. You can make the sauce in advance but, for best results, cook the fish just before serving.

8 x 200g portions fresh kingklip

Marinade for kingklip

60ml (4T) fresh lime juice
10ml (2t) pared or finely grated
   lime rind
3ml (½t) dried chilli flakes
125ml (½ cup) Hamilton Russell
   Vineyards Extra-virgin Olive Oil

Parsley crème fraîche sauce

125ml (½ cup) flat-leaf parsley,
   leaves only, finely chopped
250g (500ml) crème fraîche
10ml (2t) fresh lime juice
3ml (½t) finely grated lime rind

Serves 8

Kingklip

1. Mix all the marinade ingredients together.
2. Place the fish portions in a glass or ceramic dish. Pour over the marinade and leave for 20–30 minutes.
3. Preheat a large frying pan (or two, if necessary). Remove the fish from the marinade but do not drain, as the oil is sufficient to fry the fish. Cook for 3 minutes on one side and 2 minutes on the other side.
   Serve immediately, with the parsley sauce spooned over.

Parsley crème fraîche sauce

1. In a small bowl, combine the chopped parsley with all the other ingredients.
   Set aside until needed, or place overnight in the fridge in an airtight container.

COOK'S NOTES

- Instead of kingklip, you can use any mild-flavoured, flaky, white fish.
- Serve any extra sauce on the side.

WINE SUGGESTIONS

Choose a subtly oaked white wine that can stand up to the earthy beetroot notes and pungent cardamon aromas.
- Rhone style white blend (incorporating Viognier) from the Swartland district, Western Cape.
- Chateauneuf-du-Pape Blanc from a reputable Chateau (Rhône region, France).
- Condrieu; choose a top producer of this classy 100% Viognier wine from the Rhône Valley.

For Beetroot and cardamom pap, see page 92.

Beetroot and cardamom pap with edamame beans

This is a lovely fusion of traditional African and Asian ingredients. 'Pap', a firm-textured starch made from coarsely ground maize meal, is an African staple. In this dish, it is combined with edamame beans, which feature in many Japanese dishes.

375ml (1½ cups) water
125ml (½ cup) beetroot juice (*see* Cook's notes)
3ml (½ t) fine table salt
375ml (1½ cups) coarsely ground maize meal
250ml (1 cup) cold water
120g butter
3–4 cardamom pods
10ml (2t) Hamilton Russell Vineyards Extra-virgin Olive Oil
160g fresh edamame beans (*see* Cook's notes)

Serves 8

1. In a medium-sized pot, bring 375ml (1½ cups) water to the boil, then add the beetroot juice and salt.
2. Mix the maize meal with 250ml (1 cup) cold water, and slowly add to the boiling water, whisking continuously to prevent lumps from forming.
3. Lower the heat and leave to simmer for 15 minutes with the lid on, plus 15 minutes with the lid off, stirring every 5 minutes. As the maize meal cooks, it will thicken and become porridge-like.
4. Cut the butter into blocks and stir into the maize meal 'pap'.
5. Crush the cardamom pods in a pestle and mortar, remove the husks and fry the seeds in the olive oil for 1 minute. Add to the pap.
6. Boil the edamame beans in lightly salted water for 5 minutes. Drain, and add to the pap.

To serve
For Valentine's Day, I use individual heart-shaped moulds, but any shape will do. Brush the moulds with a little olive oil and spoon in the hot pap. Smooth the top and turn out onto the plate immediately.

COOK'S NOTES
- For 125ml (½ cup) beetroot juice you need about 250g fresh, uncooked beetroot. Trim and scrub the beetroot (there is no need to peel) and juice in a juicer.
- You can subsitute the pap with polenta (finely ground maize meal). Follow the cooking instructions on the packet. When the poltena pulls away from the pan, add the butter, cardamom seeds and edamame beans.
- Edamame are immature 'green' soybeans in the pod. Fresh edamame are normally boiled in salted water and served whole, or eaten by squeezing the beans out of the pods. Salt or other seasonings may be added. If you can't get fresh edamame beans, use the frozen variety.

Fig and pistachio tart
with Sauvignon Blanc sorbet

In late summer, when the grapes hang heavy on the vines and the scent of ripening figs permeates the air, I get an irresistible urge to make this luscious tart. I serve it with a sorbet made from our own Sauvignon Blanc grapes, but it tastes just as good made with white table grapes.

Sweet pastry

120g butter
75g icing sugar
2 egg yolks
250g cake flour, sifted

Fig and pistachio filling

200g butter
200g icing sugar
2 eggs
150g unsalted pistachio nuts,
  shelled, peeled and chopped
  (*see* Cook's notes, page 98)
50g (6T) cake flour, sifted
8 ripe figs, washed and quartered
30ml (2T) icing sugar, for sifting
45ml (3T) melted Hamilton Russell
  Vineyards Fynbos Honey

Serves 8

Sweet pastry

1. In a food processor or mixer, cream the butter and icing sugar.
2. Add the egg yolks, one by one, and mix until smooth and creamy.
3. Add all the flour at once, and mix just until it comes together.
4. Transfer the pastry to a sheet of cling wrap, shape into a ball, wrap tightly and place in the fridge to rest for 30 minutes.
5. Spray a 26cm loose-based tart tin with non-stick cooking spray.
6. Sprinkle some icing sugar on a clean work surface. Unwrap the chilled pastry, flatten slightly and roll out to a diameter of 18–20cm.
7. Lift the pastry onto the rolling pin and unroll it into the tin. Press the pastry evenly into the base and sides of the tin, making sure it is no thicker than 2mm. Trim the edges, cover with cling wrap and rest in the fridge for 15 minutes.
8. Preheat the oven to 150°C.
9. Remove the pastry case from the fridge, uncover and prick the base with a fork.
10. Line the pastry case with baking paper (making sure the sides are covered), fill with baking beans and blind bake for 30 minutes. Set aside to cool.

Fig and pistachio filling

1. Preheat the oven to 180°C.
2. In a food processor or mixer, cream the butter and icing sugar.
3. Add the eggs and, when fully incorporated, add the chopped pistachio nuts and flour.
4. Smooth the filling over the pastry base.
5. Arrange the fig quarters on top and sift over the icing sugar.
6. Bake for about 30 minutes, until golden brown.
7. As soon as the tart comes out of the oven, drizzle over the melted honey, starting at the centre of the tart and pouring in an outward spiral. Leave to cool before removing the tart from the tin.

For Sauvignon Blanc sorbet, Cook's notes and Wine suggestions, see page 98.

Sauvignon Blanc sorbet

850g ripe Sauvignon Blanc grapes, destalked, rinsed and drained (*see* Cook's notes)
10ml (2t) fresh lemon juice
5ml (1t) melted Hamilton Russell Vineyards Fynbos Honey

1. Purée the grapes in a liquidizer or food processor, or crush by hand.
2. Strain through a sieve to remove the skins and pips, pressing with a wooden spoon to extract as much juice as possible.
3. Add the lemon juice and melted honey to the grape juice, and freeze in an ice-cream machine.

To serve
Cut the Fig and pistachio tart (*see* page 96) into slices and serve with a scoop of sorbet.

COOK'S NOTES
- You can substitute fresh figs with dried figs that have been rehydrated in rooibos tea. Use two teabags per litre of boiling water and steep the figs for 20–30 minutes (soft-dried figs need only 10 minutes or so).
- Use white table grapes in place of Sauvignon Blanc grapes.
- About 850g (6 bunches) of grapes should give you enough juice.
- To skin pistachio nuts, bring a small pot of water to a boil. Add the shelled pistachios, and boil for 1–2 minutes or until the skins are softened. Drain, and place on a clean towel. Rub the nuts with the towel until their skins pop off.
- The pastry case can be made the day before and blind baked, then wrapped in foil or cling wrap and stored at room temperature until needed. Only fill the pastry case just before baking, to prevent it from becoming soggy.
- Fynbos honey tends to crystalize within three months of bottling, so it needs to be melted before use. You can use any variety of honey, as long as it is runny enough to drizzle over the warm figs.

WINE SUGGESTIONS
A botrytized wine made from Sauvignon Blanc or Semillon will be the logical pairing here.
- Noble Late Harvest Sauvignon Blanc from Stellenbosch, Western Cape.
- Barsac (a Sauvignon Blanc, Sémillon, Muscadelle blend) from the Sauternes region, France.
- For a really special occasion, choose a top-notch Sauternes, one of the world's iconic sweet wines.

Autumn

The harvest comes to an end; it's been a good year, and the hard work in the vineyards has been worthwhile.

RIGHT Horrocks, one of our Great Danes, on his daybed in front of the kitchen hearth.

FAR RIGHT In the vineyards, the first autumnal leaves start to appear.

March

This is the final push towards completing the harvest. The later vineyards use the last of their energy to bring their berries to perfect ripeness. In the vineyards that have already been harvested, gold and yellow autumnal leaves start to appear here and there in the canopies. The best wines are made 'on the margin' and the vines just get their job done; their load was in balance with their ability. Those vineyards that have served well and for long enough are removed as soon as the grapes come off. The vines have been there for many years and the soil must rest and recover before being prepared for replanting in two to three years. Other things will grow there for a while and add back to the land. A tired vineyard team completes the harvest in the last week of the month.

The cellar team is weary too, but enthused. It has been a great year, with a warm, dry, January followed by a cooler and drier than average February. Their hours have been dictated by the grapes and the wines and it shows. De-stemming, pressing, settling, barrel-filling, pumping over and punching down, measuring, monitoring, analyzing, tasting and cleaning, always cleaning. The cellar is awash with the invigorating smell of fermenting wine; there's beauty in the making. A winemaker's life is measured in these annual bursts of extreme application, and this peak level of activity will not be over for a while.

Just as the grape harvest draws to a close, the olives announce their approaching readiness. Here and there in the groves, the earlier olives show hints of darkening on their now yellow-green skins. They will be hand-picked before they are fully black and ripe. Olives on the greener side of fully ripe ensure the vibrant, fresh, peppery characters that make extra-virgin olive oil such a beautiful, even indispensable, accompaniment to so many dishes. Greener olives give much less oil, but it is a better oil, with far more impact.

The fynbos looks tired as well. It offers so much magnificence for most of the year, but now it is dry. It is time to walk the cliff path along the rocky edge of Walker Bay. In the cool morning, the heady 'kelp and iodine' smell of the sea combines with the deep bass of the big swell to hint at a presence: unstoppable, ancient and ever so slightly sinister – just enough to invigorate the senses. Our Estate's giant, free air-conditioner is always there. There is nothing but sea from here to Antarctica, far to the south. And, in the dark stony soil on either side of the cliff path, the occasional blood flower (*Haemanthus coccineus*) bursts from the ground, a bright, vibrant arterial red. March is a tired month, but still very much alive.

Mushroom risotto

After the first heavy autumn rains, it only takes a sunny day or two before mushrooms start popping up all over the pine forest. Foraged wild mushrooms have a rich earthiness which balances beautifully with the subtle flavours of cultivated mushrooms. If you are not able to obtain all the mushrooms listed, buy as many different varieties as you can.

60ml (¼ cup) Hamilton Russell Vineyards Extra-virgin Olive Oil

70g shiitake mushrooms, finely chopped

120g portabellini mushrooms, finely chopped

50g king oyster mushrooms, finely chopped

50g each brown and white shimeji mushrooms, separated

30ml (2T) Bovril or Marmite (*see* Cook's notes)

500ml (2 cups) chicken stock

500ml (2 cups) vegetable stock

30ml (2T) mushroom powder (*see* Cook's notes)

15ml (1T) dark soy sauce

50g butter

1 medium red onion, chopped

15ml (1T) fresh garlic, chopped

500g risotto rice

125ml Hamilton Russell Vineyards Pinot Noir (*see* Cook's notes)

200ml (¾ cup) mature Klein River Gruyère Cheese, finely grated, plus extra, for serving

80ml (⅓ cup) fresh cream

5ml (1t) white truffle oil

brown and white shimeji mushrooms, for garnish

deep-fried sage leaves, for garnish

Serves 8

1. Heat 45ml (3T) olive oil in a medium-sized pan. Add all the mushrooms. Fry for about 3 minutes, until the mushrooms start to soften.
2. Stir in 15ml (1T) Bovril or Marmite. Remove from the heat and set aside, keeping warm.
3. In a separate pot, combine the chicken and vegetable stock and heat to simmering.
4. Add the mushroom powder, soy sauce and remaining spoon of Bovril or Marmite. Stir to combine. Keep warm but do not allow to boil.
5. In a large pot, heat the remaining olive oil and melt the butter. Add the onion and garlic and fry until the onion becomes glossy and translucent.
6. Add the risotto rice and continue to fry until the grains of rice are coated in the buttery sauce (about 2 minutes).
7. Add the wine and stir gently until all the wine is absorbed (this will take about 1 minute). Turn the heat down to low.
8. As soon as the wine has been absorbed by the rice add a ladle-full of stock. When this has been absorbed (about 30 seconds), add another ladle-full. Continue adding stock, one ladle-full at a time, until all the stock has been used. Each ladle-full will take a touch longer to be absorbed (up to 7 minutes towards the end) but don't be tempted to add more stock until the last lot has been absorbed. Gently stir the rice occasionally to ensure it does not burn, but don't overdo it, or the rice will become porridge-like. It is important to keep the heat very low.
9. When all the stock has been absorbed, add the fried mushrooms, Gruyère cheese, cream and truffle oil and stir gently through the rice.

To serve

Serve in individual bowls, topped with fresh shimeji mushrooms and deep-fried sage leaves. Drizzle with extra-virgin olive oil and pass around some finely grated Gruyère cheese for guests to help themselves.

COOK'S NOTES

- For a vegetarian version, use Marmite or Vegemite instead of Bovril, and substitute the chicken stock with additional vegetable stock.
- **Mushroom powder** I use a variety of mushrooms from the estate: cow bolete or slippery jacks (*Suillus bovinus*), pine bolete (*Boletus pinophilus*) and ceps or porcini (*Boletus edulis*). Gently wipe the mushrooms to remove any pine needles, leaves and traces of soil. Cut them into 1cm-thick slices and place on an oven rack covered in perforated foil. Set the oven to 60°C and leave the mushrooms to dry overnight (wedging the oven door slightly open with a wooden spoon helps to increase air circulation). Once the slices are fully dried, I use a coffee grinder to powder them. Mushroom powder will keep for up to 12 months in an airtight container. Alternatively, buy dried porcini mushrooms and grind them to a fine powder.
- If you want to gather edible wild mushrooms, you must use a reputable field guide applicable to your area, or go with someone who knows what they are doing. Never eat any mushroom you can't positively identify as safe for consumption.
- I use Klein River cheese, which is made in Stanford, but any mature Gruyère or Parmesan-style cheese can be used.
- Pinot Noir is the ideal wine to use for this risotto, as it has a natural affinity with mushrooms.

WINE SUGGESTIONS

A powerful yet delicate and lively red will highlight the earthy flavours of the medley of mushrooms.

- Pinot Noir from the Hemel-en-Aarde Valley.
- Gevrey Chambertin Premier Cru, a top-notch, intensely flavoured Pinot Noir from Burgundy.
- Barolo or Barbaresco, Nebbiolo-based wines from Piedmont, northern Italy.

Each month brings new foraging opportunities in the fields, forests and fynbos of the Estate.

LEFT The stone pines provide plenty of pine nuts, which we use for homemade pesto.

RIGHT Wild rocket has a lovely peppery taste and is lovely in salads.

LEFT Agatha, our the octogenarian leopard tortoise, catches some morning sunshine.

RIGHT Fragrant lemon verbena grows in the herb garden.

Lime-marinated Cape salmon
with stuffed courgette flowers

8 x 150g portions of Cape salmon
45ml (3T) fresh lime juice
10ml (2t) finely grated lime rind
10ml (2t) fresh marjoram leaves
125ml (½ cup) Hamilton Russell
   Vineyards Extra-virgin Olive Oil
fresh lemon slices, for garnish
flaked sea salt, for garnish

Serves 8

1. Place the fish portions in an ovenproof dish.
2. Mix the lime juice and rind, herbs and olive oil and spoon over the fish.
3. Leave to marinade for 20–30 minutes. (Place in the fridge on a hot day.)
4. Preheat the oven to 180°C and bake for 20–25 minutes.

To serve Garnish with lemon slices and flaked sea salt. Serve with stuffed courgette flowers (*see* page 110).

COOK'S NOTES
- Cape salmon (geelbek) has firm, white, flesh and is ideal for baking, grilling or pan-frying. Any other firm-fleshed fish can be substituted.
- My fail-safe method to testing if fish is cooked is to insert the tip of a sharp knife into the thickest part of the flesh and hold it there for 5 seconds. If the knife comes out hot, the fish is cooked.

WINE SUGGESTIONS
This delicate dish needs a lively, peppery, white wine with a mineral structure.
- Sauvignon Blanc from Walker Bay, Western Cape.
- Bordeaux Blanc Sec (a Sauvignon Blanc-Semillon blend) from the Bordeaux region, France.
- Rueda, an aromatic wine made from the Verdejo grape; from Spain.

Salad of rocket, sorrel, courgette, radish and pine nuts

A real treat, especially if you are able to make this salad using only home-grown produce.

80g wild rocket, washed
30g sorrel, washed and shredded
250ml (1 cup) courgettes, rinsed
   and diced
200ml (¾ cup) red radishes,
   washed and finely sliced
80ml (⅓ cup) Hamilton Russell
   Vineyards Extra-virgin Olive Oil
salt and pepper, to taste
125ml (½ cup) pine nuts
fresh rocket flowers, for garnish

1. Gently toss the rocket, sorrel, courgettes, radishes and olive oil together. Season to taste.
2. Toast the pine nuts in a non-stick pan, shaking the pan frequently to prevent them from burning. Cool slightly, then sprinkle over the salad.
3. Garnish with yellow rocket flowers.

COOK'S NOTES
- No lemon juice is required in the salad, as the sorrel has a lovely acidity.
- There is no need to use oil when toasting the pine nuts.
- If you don't have rocket flowers, simply omit them.
- Bought wild rocket comes in 80g and 30g packs.
- If you can't get sorrel, substitute baby or English spinach and add 25ml (1½T) lemon juice.

For Stuffed courgette flowers, see page 110.

Stuffed courgette flowers

Courgettes, or baby marrows, belong to the summer squash family. They are easy and rewarding to grow. The flowers, which bloom from late summer to early autumn, can be used fresh in salads or stuffed and deep-fried.

150g cake flour, sifted
1 egg, separated
80ml (⅓ cup) white wine
30ml (2T) Hamilton Russell
    Vineyards Extra-virgin Olive Oil
16 courgette flowers
80g pine nuts
500g cream cheese
125ml (½ cup) sparkling water, at
    room temperature
250ml (1 cup) olive or canola oil,
    for frying

Serves 8

1. Make a batter by mixing the flour, egg yolk, wine and olive oil together in a bowl. Set aside for about 30 minutes to rest.
2. While the batter is resting, trim the flowers, carefully cutting out the stamens. Rinse under cold water and set aside to dry.
3. Gently crush the pine nuts in a pestle and mortar, retaining some texture. Fold the pine nuts into the cream cheese.
4. Fill each flower with the cheese mixture and carefully twist the petals closed at the top.
5. When you are ready to fry the flowers, whisk the egg white to stiff peaks.
6. Add the sparkling water to the batter and whisk until smooth and runny.
7. Gently fold the egg white into the batter.
8. Heat the olive or canola oil in a small pan.
9. Dip each flower in the batter, ensuring it is well coated. Fry in batches, turning, until the batter becomes crisp and turns light gold (this will initially take about 3 minutes per side, but takes less time as the oil gets hotter). Drain the finished flowers on paper towel.

To serve Serve with Lime-marinated Cape salmon (*see* page 108).

COOK'S NOTES

- It is important to remove the stamens and stems as these are rather bitter.
- When dipping the flowers in the batter, hold them over the batter for a couple of seconds to allow the excess to drip off.
- Instead of courgette flowers, deep-fry courgette ribbons, and serve the cream cheese stuffing on the side.
- If you pick the courgette flowers from your garden, make sure the plants have not been recently sprayed with any chemicals.

Mango and lemon-scented geranium sorbet
on lemon verbena shortbread

Sweet tropical mangoes are packed with anti-oxidants, and the flavours are beautifully lifted by the fresh notes of lemon-scented geranium (Pelargonium citronellum) and lemon verbena.

Mango sorbet

1kg fresh mango, cubed
300g castor sugar
60ml (¼ cup) fresh lemon juice
15ml (1T) fresh lime juice
3 lemon-scented geranium leaves, washed

Lemon verbena shortbread

200g cake flour
100g cornflour
1ml (⅛t) salt
250g butter
100g lemon verbena-flavoured castor sugar (*see* Cook's notes), plus extra for sprinkling

fresh geranium flowers or leaves, for garnish

Serves 8

Mango and lemon-scented geranium sorbet

1. Purée the mango flesh in a food processor.
2. Add the castor sugar and continue mixing until the sugar has dissolved.
3. Add the remaining ingredients and blend for another minute.
4. Transfer to an ice cream machine to freeze.
5. Just before the sorbet freezes hard, transfer to eight loose-based tart tins (± 7cm diameter). Return to the freezer.

Lemon verbena shortbread

1. Preheat the oven to 190°C.
2. Sift the flour, cornflour and salt twice.
3. Using an electric mixer, cream the butter until light and fluffy, then add the flavoured castor sugar, one tablespoon at a time, while beating continuously.
4. Add the flour mixture and work it in with your fingertips until a stiff dough forms.
5. Spray a 24 x 33cm baking tray with non-stick cooking spray and press the dough into it.
6. Smooth the top and mark out eight rounds the same diameter as the tart tins, but do not cut all the way through. Use a fork to pierce holes in the dough in an even pattern. Sprinkle lightly with extra castor sugar.
7. Bake until golden, but not brown (± 10–15 minutes). Remove from the oven and gently cut through the pieces. Leave to cool in the pan.

To serve

Unmould the sorbet and serve on top of a shortbread biscuit. Garnish with a fresh geranium flower or leaf.

COOK'S NOTES

- It is unusual to use lemon and lime juice in the same dish, as lemon suggests Mediterranean flavours and lime suggests Mexican but here, the combination really does add to the flavour.
- Instead of lemon-scented geranium leaves, use two lemon verbena leaves or 3ml (½t) freshly grated lime rind.
- To make lemon verbena sugar, add 15ml (1T) chopped lemon verbena leaves to 100g castor sugar and store in an airtight container for at least a week. Or simply blend the lemon verbena leaves and castor sugar in a food processor until the leaves are very fine (this will add both colour and flavour to the shortbread).
- *Pelargoniums*, commonly known as scented geraniums or storksbills, are indigenous to South Africa. *Pelargonium citronellum* (lemon-scented geranium) is widely grown in gardens. It is an evergreen, bushy shrub, with strongly lemon-scented leaves, that flowers during spring and summer.

WINE SUGGESTIONS

Freshness is the key word here, so choose a wine with just the right amount of sugar and bracing acidity.
- Mosel Riesling, Beerenauslese ('late harvest') style, around 5 years old; from Germany.

ABOVE AND RIGHT On weekends, we often walk along the cliff path in Hermanus, where the blood flower (*Haemanthus coccineus*) is in bloom at this time of year.

FAR RIGHT Our olives are picked green to enhance the aromas and the intense peppery flavours of the oil.

The fresh cut grass and apple aromas of the first olive oil is something unforgettable that marks the season for us.

April

There is dew on the grass in the cool mornings now and a chill to the early evenings. The vineyards are gently sliding into their winter sleep. The first of the bigger rains arrive on schedule, enough to soften the stony ground for new vineyard preparation. We leave an open field alongside new vineyards; a 'biodiversity island' of several species of beneficial plants to harbour the natural predators of vineyard pests. The large bulldozer arrives and work begins: deep-ripping the slope to just over a metre, then cross-ploughing in two directions. If the soil is too dry it will end up blocky and poorly mixed; too wet and the heavy clay will smear, not mix. This year our timing is good. Elsewhere, the rows are prepared and the cover crop is seeded and fed. The vines have been put to bed.

The olives aren't ripe, but they are ready as we want them. It is a very small crop, hand-picked in only two days. It is pressed immediately and the first of the season's oil makes its way to the table. Cloudy, unfiltered, deep green, and smelling of freshly cut grass and apples – something unforgettable that marks the season for us.

In the barrel cellar, the last of the Chardonnay's yeast-driven alcoholic fermentations hiss on, but not for much longer. Malolactic fermentations are well underway as harder malic acid is slowly converted to softer lactic acid by beneficial bacteria. A round richness is already balancing the tight, vibrant mineral core of the wines. *Battonage* begins when malolactic fermentation ends and will continue every two weeks for a while. This gentle stirring of the spent yeast cells, or lees, back into suspension adds complexity and body while keeping the wine fresh.

The rains combine with the regular warmth of the days to bring on the mushrooms and all the pleasures of searching for them in the pine, poplar and oak forests. The first to appear are the bay bolete (*Boletus badius*), followed by poplar bolete (*Leccinum duriusculum*) and then, the one that excites us most, the cep or porcini (*Boletus edulis*); we only find a few, but they are celebrated. In the pine forest, the sticky capped cow bolete, also known as slippery jacks, (*Suillus* species) are the last to appear. We dry and powder them to use in sauces for the rest of the year.

We hold a farewell function for our assistant winemakers who will travel South Africa for a while before returning home to prepare for another harvest. They bring wines from their countries and we open a few special bottles from our cellar. It's time to thank the vineyard team for another successful harvest, and we host a party for them. A pair of spotted eagle owls call to each other near the house just after sunset; a good omen. A half moon is up and there is an orange glow low in the west.

Ravioli of venison biltong and mushrooms
in a creamy mushroom sauce

This is a wonderfully meaty 'mushroomy' dish with lots of umami!

Venison biltong and mushroom filling

30ml (2T) Hamilton Russell Vineyards Extra-virgin Olive Oil

160g portabellini mushrooms, finely chopped

10ml (2t) mushroom powder (*see* Cook's notes)

10ml (2t) Bovril

50g venison biltong, powdered (*see* Cook's notes)

Creamy mushroom sauce

15ml (1T) Hamilton Russell Vineyards Extra-virgin Olive Oil

50g brown shimeji mushrooms, separated

5ml (1t) Bovril

1 litre (4 cups) fresh cream

35g dried porcini mushrooms, chopped

10ml (2t) pickled jalapeño chillies, chopped

10ml (2t) dark soy sauce

25ml (1½T) teriyaki sauce

10ml (2t) mushroom powder (*see* Cook's notes)

2ml (¼t) sesame oil

Handmade ravioli

300g cake flour, sifted

100g semolina, sifted

4 eggs

olive oil, for cooking

salt, for cooking

fresh sage leaves, for garnish

Serves 8

Venison biltong and mushroom filling

1. Heat the olive oil in a medium frying pan. Add the portabellini mushrooms, mushroom powder and Bovril.
2. Fry over a high heat for 5 minutes, until all the pan juices have evaporated.
3. Remove from the heat and set aside to cool, then stir in the powdered venison biltong.

Creamy mushroom sauce

1. Heat the olive oil in a medium saucepan. Add the shimeji mushrooms and Bovril and fry gently until the mushrooms are soft and most of the liquid has evaporated. Set aside.
2. Pour the cream into a clean saucepan or small pot. Add the dried porcini mushrooms, jalapeño chillies, soy sauce, teriyaki sauce, mushroom powder and sesame oil.
3. When the cream comes to the boil, lower the heat. Add the reserved shimeji mushrooms and simmer for about 10 minutes to reduce and concentrate the sauce.
4. Remove from the heat and set aside, covered, until needed. Reheat gently before serving.

Handmade ravioli

1. Place the cake flour, semolina and eggs in the bowl of an electric mixer.
2. Using the dough hook, mix on medium speed until an homogenous mix has been achieved.
3. Still using the mixer, knead the dough until it becomes smooth and forms a firm ball. It should not be sticky, if it is, add a little extra semolina. (If you can't knead the dough into a firm ball in the mixer, tip it onto a floured work surface and knead by hand.)
4. When the dough stops sticking to the bowl or the work surface, shape it into three or four fist-sized balls and tightly wrap each one in cling wrap.
5. Leave to stand at room temperature for about 30 minutes, to allow the gluten to relax. (Don't leave it for much longer than this.)

Preparing and cooking the ravioli
See pages 86–87.

To serve
Arrange five ravioli pockets on a plate and spoon over some warm sauce. Garnish with fresh sage leaves and serve immediately.

COOK'S NOTES
- Mushroom powder can be made from dried porcini mushrooms (*Boletus edulis*), also known as porcini or ceps (*see* page 104).
- Powdered biltong is widely available but, to make your own, grind thin slices of venison or beef biltong in a coffee grinder or processor. Use biltong that is not too salty.
- You can make the ravioli up to two weeks ahead and place it in the freezer. Layer the parcels between sheets of baking paper in an airtight container, making sure the edges don't touch. Cook directly from frozen.
- To make the pasta dough by hand: mound the flour on a clean, flat work surface. Make a well in the centre and crack in the eggs, then use a fork to slowly mix the eggs into the flour. Once the egg and flour mixture is combined, start kneading, and follow the method above.

WINE SUGGESTIONS
The combination of gamey venison, earthy mushrooms and fresh sage call for a red wine that is bold and full of personality.
- Mourvèdre from Walker Bay, Western Cape.
- Bandol (at least 7 years old); this Mourvedre-based wine comes from Provence, France
- Brunello di Montalcino, an iconic, sought-after wine from Tuscany, Italy; this wine ages well, so choose one that is at least 9 years old.

As the mornings and evenings get cooler, we make the most of April's sunny days.

LEFT AND RIGHT Succulent sour figs (*Carpobrotus* spp.) grow in the coastal sand dunes of the southwestern Cape. Some have yellow flowers, others have pink or magenta flowers. The fresh fruits are made into jams and preserves and the sap was traditionally used as an antiseptic. The dried fruits, known as 'suurvye' are a local delicacy.

LEFT One of our Great Danes, Ophelia, enjoying the afternoon sun on the loggia.

RIGHT Looking down on the tasting room from the pine forest.

Baby sole baked in a creamy lemon-shrimp sauce
topped with capelin caviar

Baked baby sole

16 baby soles
100g (8T) butter
60ml (4T) fresh lemon juice
30ml (2T) freshly grated lemon zest

Creamy lemon-shrimp sauce

750ml (3 cups) cream
360g shrimps, peeled and cleaned
45ml (3T) fresh lemon juice
15ml (3t) rice vinegar

capelin caviar, to garnish (*see* Cook's notes)

Serves 8

Baked baby sole

1. Preheat the oven to 180°C. Line two roasting pans with foil and place 8 baby soles in each.
2. Dot with butter, drizzle over the lemon juice and sprinkle lemon zest evenly over the soles. Cover with foil and bake for 30–40 minutes, until cooked (To test if fish is cooked, insert the tip of a sharp knife into the thickest part of the fish and hold it there for 5 seconds. If the knife comes out hot, the fish is cooked. Start testing after 30 minutes.)

Creamy lemon-shrimp sauce

1. In a medium saucepan, bring the cream to the boil then turn down the heat. Simmer for 5 minutes then remove from the heat.
2. Add the shrimps, lemon juice and rice vinegar and purée with a hand-held blender.
3. Return the sauce to a low heat and simmer gently for 20 minutes, or until the sauce has reduced by about a quarter. Stir regularly and do not allow the sauce to boil over. Keep warm until needed.

To serve

Allow two baby soles per person. Spoon over some sauce and top with a dollop of capelin caviar. Accompany with potato, pea and fennel mash.

COOK'S NOTES

*   If you can't get baby soles, use one standard sole per person. The cooking time will depend on the thickness of the soles, and whether you can fit two roasting trays into the oven.
*   If you use frozen shrimps, thaw them, then rinse, drain and pat dry before adding to the cream.
*   Capelin caviar is naturally vivid orange in colour, although it is also dyed red or black. If you can't obtain it, use any orange-coloured caviar or roe. Capelin caviar is used extensively in sushi. (In Japan, it is sold under the name 'masago'.)
*   Several species of flatfish belong to the Soleidae family. East Coast Sole (*Austroglossus pectoralis*) is endemic to the South African coast. Sole are on the SASSI orange (caution) list, so although sole is delicious, enjoy it as a special treat.
*   Always use foil with the shiny side facing the food.

WINE SUGGESTIONS

A citrussy, crunchy, mineral-laden, unoaked white wine will be perfect with this delicate fish dish.

*   Verdelho (a flavoursome, fruity wine, originally from Portugal) from Bot River, Western Cape.
*   Bone-dry Riesling from Alsace, France.
*   Vouvray Sec (a dry Chenin Blanc) from France's Loire Valley.

Potato, pea and fennel mash

140g baby fennel (bulbs and stalks), rinsed and trimmed
30ml (2T) Hamilton Russell Vineyards Extra-virgin Olive Oil
1kg potatoes, rinsed and diced
1½ litres (6 cups) boiling water
3ml (½t) salt
45g butter
80ml (⅓ cup) fresh cream
300g fresh or frozen peas
750ml (3 cups) boiling water
3ml (½t) salt

1. Preheat the oven to 150°C.
2. Lay the fennel on a roasting tray, drizzle with olive oil and roast for 20 minutes. Leave to cool, then chop finely.
3. Meanwhile, boil the potatoes in salted water until soft, about 30 minutes. Drain well. Add the butter and cream and mash by hand until smooth. Set aside and keep warm.
4. Boil the peas in salted water for 5 minutes. Drain and purée with a hand-held blender.
5. Combine the mashed potatoes, chopped fennel and puréed peas. Reheat gently before serving.

COOK'S NOTES

*   One kilogram of potatoes should yield about 10 medium potatoes.
*   Do not use a blender or food processor to mash potatoes; they will become sticky and stringy.
*   140g baby fennel is about five lengths of fennel stalks with bulbs attached.

Olive oil ice cream with sour fig syrup

The first green-golden olive oil of the season is a precious treat! This recipe is inspired by the olive oil gelato served at Mario Batali's Babbo, one of our favourite New York restaurants. In Italy, vanilla ice cream is sometimes served with a drizzle of fresh olive oil and a sprinkling of flaked sea salt, and olive oil ice cream is almost always served with a little salt. Sour figs (Carpobrotus spp.) are an easy-to-grow, succulent groundcover with edible fruit, which has a sweet-salty flavour, making it a lovely local substitute for salt in this dish.

100g castor sugar

45ml (3T) honey

6 egg yolks

2ml (¼t) vanilla paste

125ml (½ cup) Hamilton Russell Vineyards Extra-virgin Olive Oil (*see* Cook's notes)

750ml (3 cups) milk (*see* Cook's notes)

250ml (1 cup) fresh cream

sour fig syrup, to serve (*see* Cook's notes)

Makes about 1 litre

Serves 8

1. Combine the castor sugar, honey, egg yolks and vanilla paste in the bowl of an electric mixer and beat for about 5 minutes on medium speed until very pale yellow and fluffy.
2. Add the olive oil in a steady stream, while beating continuously. When all the oil has been added, continue to beat for 2 minutes.
3. Add the milk and beat for 2 minutes
4. Add the cream and beat for a further 2 minutes.
5. Transfer the mixture to a heavy-based pot and heat just until it starts to boil, stirring continuously. (Do not let it boil as this will cause the custard to curdle and separate.)
6. Transfer the custard to a metal bowl and immerse the base in an ice bath to stop it cooking any further. Stir occasionally until cooled (±15 minutes), then transfer to an ice-cream machine to churn and freeze.
7. Just before the ice cream becomes hard-frozen, transfer it to a mould or suitable container. Cover and freeze for at least 2 hours or overnight.

To serve
Place a scoop or two of ice cream in a bowl and drizzle with sour fig syrup.

COOK'S NOTES
- It is very important to use fresh, extra-virgin olive oil in this recipe. Buy locally made olive oil and make sure it comes from the current vintage.
- **Sour fig syrup** The fruit of sour figs (*Carpobrotus* spp.) becomes yellow and fragrant when ripe, with the outer skin turning wrinkly and rubbery as they dry (*see* page 120). Soak the dried fruits in hot water for about 5 minutes, cut the stalks off and squeeze out the sticky syrup and seeds. About 400g of dried sour figs ('suurvye') will yield 120ml syrup. Store any extra syrup in a jar in the fridge for about 6 months
- You can substitute the sour fig syrup with a sprinkling of flaked sea salt.
- If you don't have an ice-cream machine, use good quality vanilla ice cream. Soften it enough to scoop into a mould, then freeze. Serve drizzled with fresh olive oil and sour fig syrup or a sprinkling of flaked sea salt.
- I prefer to use fat-free milk for this ice cream, as I find full-cream milk is too rich.

WINE SUGGESTIONS
A sweet fortified wine with grapey notes will stand up to the olive oil and sour figs.
- White Jerepigo-style wine (made from muscat grapes), served on crushed ice, with a lime wedge on the side.
- Muscat de Rivesaltes, a fortified *vin doux naturel* from the Roussillon region of southern France.

This is a lovely month
for picnics and long
walks with the dogs.

ABOVE The regular southeast
breezes coming directly off
the bay provide a perfect
opportunity for paragliding
above the ridge.

RIGHT Relaxing in the garden
with a glass of Pinot Noir.

FAR RIGHT Olive's studio, built
with the local sandstone,
blends into the fynbos.

May

The vines were put to bed in April and this month they must fall asleep. A good early dormancy, and a complete one, ensures a timely and even bud-break in Spring. We need at least a week of minimum overnight temperatures below 9°C for deep sleep. Being so close to the sea benefits us with cooler summers, but it can hurt us with warmer autumns and winters. Not this year though. We get our week of cold nights early in the month.

There is more rain, too, and in the vineyards, the green tips of the cover crop begin to show between the rows. The team is working on the trellising for the young vines in their second year. Farm implements are repaired and serviced and it's a good time to assess the lessons of the harvest. The wines from the trials and experiments, although unfinished, can now be tasted for insight.

Battonage continues in the cellar along with analytical tastings of the numerous 'parcels' of wine which will make up the final blends. The progress of the malolactic fermentations is monitored and, in certain parcels, if our tastings raise any concerns, the health of the lees is assessed for possible removal through racking.

In the forest of radiata pines across the dam in front of the cellars, the first pine ring mushrooms (*Lactarius deliciosus*) appear alongside the sticky boletes. Their washed orange gills and caps, tinged with the greens of tarnished copper, seem to match the damp bed of needles under the trees, as if they have always belonged there. And along the Raed-na-Gael ridge behind the house, the *Protea repens* are in full bloom. Their ivory coloured flowers, tinged with light pink on some bushes, hold sugary water, a mix of rain and nectar, giving them a shiny glaze at their base and providing a feast for the long-tailed Cape sugarbirds and the brightly plumed orange-breasted sunbirds alike.

This is a month of travel for us and we exchange entertaining at home for entertaining, and being entertained, abroad. We visit distributors and customers in several countries, bringing our total number of flights for the year up to 33. By the end of the month, we will have been away from home for 25 per cent of the year thus far and flown a total of 120,000 kilometres. Although our wines are made on a small Estate near the southern tip of the African continent, they are enjoyed by people all over the world, and we are grateful for it.

Fairfield fallow deer sausage
with porcini pap and porcini cream sauce

Cecil John Rhodes introduced fallow deer to South Africa in the late 1800s. They are still found in abundance on Fairfield farm, near Napier in the southern Cape. The van der Byl family have owned this expansive property for over three centuries and members of the Hamilton Russell family have had many memorable visits there in the last 75 years. Culling, by means of hunting, becomes necessary in mid- to late autumn, when the stags start rutting. Mrs Lotti van der Byl recommends using juniper berries in fallow deer recipes, as the berries work deliciously well with the strongly flavoured meat. I like to serve this sausage as a starter with pap (a polenta-like dish made from maize meal) and a creamy mushroom sauce; a different approach to a very traditional dish!

Fallow deer sausage
500g fallow deer meat, trimmed
25g fat (*see* Cook's notes)
3ml (½t) sage
2ml (¼t) rosemary
3 juniper berries, crushed in a
  pestle and mortar
2ml (¼t) coriander seeds, crushed
  in a pestle and mortar
pinch each of ground nutmeg,
  ground cloves and cayenne
  pepper
1–2 sausage casings (*see* Cook's
  notes)

Porcini pap
1 litre (4 cups) water
125ml (½ cup) dried porcini
  mushrooms, finely chopped
pinch of table salt
500ml (2 cups) maize (mealie) meal
30g (3T) butter

Porcini cream sauce
1 litre (4 cups) fresh cream
40g dried porcini mushrooms,
  chopped
10ml (2t) pickled jalapeño chillies,
  chopped
10ml (2t) dark soy sauce
30ml (2T) teriyaki sauce
20ml (4t) mushroom powder
  (*see* page 104)

sliced jalapeño chilli, for garnish
fresh rosemary flowers, for garnish

Serves 8

Fallow deer sausage
1. Chop the deer meat and fat into 2cm cubes, and mince coarsely in a meat grinder.
2. Mix all the herbs and spices together.
3. Spread the meat on a clean surface (or place in a large mixing bowl), sprinkle over the herbs and spices and work them into the meat using your hands, making sure the mixture is thoroughly combined (this should take about 3 minutes).
4. If the sausage casings have been stored in salted water, rinse well under cold fresh water. Attach the casings, one at a time, to the sausage stuffing attachment of a food processor, gathering all but about 2cm of the casing onto the nozzle.
5. Fill the funnel with meat and switch the machine on. The meat will soon appear in the casing, at which point you need to start guiding the meat off the casing at the same speed at which the sausage is filling the casing – you don't want unevenly stuffed sections. The ideal is to stuff the sausage to a diameter of ± 2cm.
6. Switch off the machine after every 20cm of sausage and twist the casing four or five times to close. (Each 20cm sausage will be one portion and you will need eight portions.)
7. To cook the sausages, pour a cup of boiling water into a large frying pan and add the sausages. Cover and poach for 2 minutes per side. Remove the lid, pour off the water and return the pan to the heat. Add a knob of butter and brown the sausages on both sides. Serve immediately.

Porcini pap
1. Pour 500ml (2 cups) water into a medium-sized pot. Add the dried porcini mushrooms and salt and bring to boil.
2. In a separate bowl, mix the maize meal with the rest of the water to make a 'porridge'.
3. Once the water in the pot has boiled for at least 2 minutes, and the dried mushrooms are properly rehydrated, stir in the maize meal 'porridge' and add the butter.
4. Reduce the heat and cook for 10 minutes, stirring occasionally. Remove from the heat.
5. Spoon the pap into eight metal panna cotta moulds or heatproof ramekins (± 110–120ml capacity). Cover the ramekins with cling wrap or foil and set aside until needed, or place in the fridge overnight.
6. To reheat before serving, uncover the moulds or ramekins and place them in a pan big enough to hold them all. Add a few centimetres of boiling water and poach for 10 minutes. (It doesn't matter if some water splashes over the pap.)

Porcini cream sauce
1. Pour the cream into a saucepan or small pot. Add the dried porcini mushrooms, jalapeño chillies, soy sauce, teriyaki sauce and mushroom powder. Heat slowly over a medium heat.
2. When it comes to the boil, lower the heat and simmer for 10 minutes or so, until reduced by about a quarter. Keep warm until required.

To serve
Unmould each serving of pap onto a plate, and serve with a portion of sausage and some porcini cream sauce spooned over. Garnish with a slice of pickled jalapeño chilli and fresh rosemary flowers.

COOK'S NOTES

- Fallow deer meat can be substituted with any lean, local venison.
- The best fat for the sausage comes from fallow deer or venison leg, but sheep or pork fat can be used instead.
- Instead of using a meat grinder, you can finely chop the meat and fat by hand, using a large chef's knife.
- Sausage casings, made from sheep's intestines, are sold by most butchers. Order them in advance.
- If you don't have a sausage stuffing machine, or a stuffing attachment for your electric mixer or food processor, you can form the meat into patties or meatballs instead.
- Making your own sausages is not difficult, but it is time-consuming. Make more than you need and freeze the rest. Fresh sausages can be safely kept in the fridge for up to 2 days, and in the freezer (preferably vacuum sealed) for up to 8 months. If you use pork fat, don't freeze the sausages for more than 2 months. Thaw frozen sausages properly before cooking.

WINE SUGGESTIONS

This dish needs a wine that can stand up to the spices in the venison, while highlighting the earthiness of the porcini.

- Mature Pinotage or Pinotage blend from Walker Bay, Western Cape.
- Ribera del Duero, a concentrated, full-bodied wine from central Spain.
- Châteauneuf-du-Pape, a blended red wine from France's Rhône region.

There are many families who have had a long association with Hamilton Russell Vineyards.

LEFT The bee team harvests the Estate's honey from one of several groups of hives placed around the property.

RIGHT Sampie has seen 32 harvests on Hamilton Russell Vineyards.

LEFT Ripe pomegranates must be harvested before the baboons get to them.

RIGHT On vacation from university, Olivia helps with entertaining overseas guests.

Franschhoek salmon trout
with kaffir lime oil

The subtle flavours and delicate texture of fresh salmon trout work splendidly with the aroma of the kaffir lime (makrut lime) leaves.

Salmon trout

8 x 100g portions of fresh
    Franschhoek salmon trout
8 fresh kaffir lime leaves, chopped
15ml (1T) Hamilton Russell
    Vineyards Extra-virgin Olive Oil
15ml (1T) fresh lime juice
45ml (3T) butter

Kaffir lime oil

125ml (½ cup) Hamilton Russell
    Vineyards Extra-virgin Olive Oil
8 fresh kaffir lime leaves, chopped

fresh kaffir lime leaves, for garnish

Serves 8

Franschhoek salmon trout

1. Place the salmon trout portions in a glass dish, skin-side down.
2. Combine the chopped kaffir lime leaves, olive oil and lime juice and spoon over the fish.
3. Cover with foil or cling wrap and leave to marinade in the fridge for 1½ hours.
4. Remove from the fridge, turn the fish over, cover again, and return to the fridge for another 1½ hours.
5. Heat the butter in a heavy-based pan. Fry the salmon trout portions, skin-side down, until the flesh turns a paler pink around the edges (this should take about 3 minutes).
6. Turn the fish over and fry for another minute. Remove the skin before serving.

Kaffir lime oil

1. Place the olive oil and kaffir lime leaves in a small saucepan and heat just until the leaves start to sizzle.
2. Remove from the heat, cover loosely and leave to stand for at least 3 hours, to allow the flavours to infuse. Strain before serving.

To serve

Drizzle some flavoured oil over the fish and garnish with fresh kaffir lime leaves, if available.
Serve with creamy pink peppercorn and cashew nut samp (*see* page 188).

COOK'S NOTES

- I use Franschhoek salmon trout, but you can use any fresh salmon or salmon trout.
- You can use dried kaffir lime leaves instead of fresh leaves, although the flavour will not be quite as 'lifted'.
- Choose a high-quality extra-virgin olive oil for cooking, as the smoke point will be higher.
- Use a glass or ceramic dish for marinating the fish, not metal, as the lime juice can cause a reaction.
- If you make the flavoured oil ahead of time, transfer it to a glass jar once cool. Store for up to one month at room temperature.

WINE SUGGESTIONS

A full-flavoured white or rosé will be a perfect match for the texture and richness of the salmon trout, and will also cut through the spicy peppercorn notes of the samp. For special occasions, choose a sparkling wine.
- Méthode Cap Classique Vintage Rosé Brut.
- Subtly oaked Semillon (at least 5 years old), from Franschhoek in the Western Cape.
- Bandol Rosé, a spicy, earthy Mourvèdre-based wine from Provence, in the south of France.

For Creamy pink peppercorn and cashew nut samp, see page 188.

Creamy pink peppercorn and cashew nut samp

This was inspired by a pink peppercorn risotto which my friend, Vicky Crease, makes. I wanted something that was a bit more African, so I've used samp (hominy), which features strongly in traditional cooking.

450g samp
1½ litres (6 cups) fresh chicken
   stock
75g finely grated mature Klein River
   Gruyére Cheese
100ml (⅖ cup) fresh cream
20ml (4t) whole pink peppercorns
100g raw (plain) cashew nuts,
   roughly chopped
35g butter
1ml (⅛t) flaked salt

1. Rinse the samp well under cold water until the water runs clear. Place in a bowl, cover with fresh cold water, and leave to soak overnight.
2. In a medium pot, bring the chicken stock to the boil. Drain the samp and add to the pot. When the stock starts boiling again, reduce the heat and simmer for about 45 minutes, until all the liquid has been absorbed.
3. Remove the pot from the heat, cover and leave to stand for 20 minutes.
4. Add the grated Gruyére cheese, cream, peppercorns, chopped cashew nuts, butter and salt and stir gently to combine. If necessary, reheat before serving, stirring gently.

To serve
Serve with Franschhoek salmon trout with kaffir lime oil (*see* page 187).

COOK'S NOTES
- Samp, also known as hominy or corn grits, is hulled corn (maize) kernels that have been stripped of their bran and germ. Instead of samp, you could substitute 450g barley or buckwheat.
- Instead of fresh chicken stock, use 30ml (2T) chicken stock powder dissolved in 1½ litres water
- If you can't get Klein River Gruyére, use any good quality, mature Gruyére or Parmesan-style cheese.

Malva pudding
with cape gooseberry custard

Malva pudding is a traditional South African dish whose origins combine our Dutch and Malay heritage. It is usually prepared with apricot preserve, but I could not resist the temptation to make a regional version. The attractive Sugarbush or Suikerbos (Protea repens) is widely distributed in the Overberg. The syrup (sap) from which the plant takes its name has been enjoyed as a sweet treat, and used medicinally, for generations, so I thought it only fitting to incorporate it in this iconic pudding.

Malva pudding

2 eggs
200g white sugar
60ml (4T) *Protea repens* syrup
   (*see* page 143)
150g cake flour
5ml (1t) bicarbonate of soda
pinch of salt
15g butter
5ml (1t) white spirit vinegar
100ml (⅖ cup) milk

Malva pudding sauce

500ml (2 cups) fresh cream
250g unsalted butter
300g white sugar
200ml (¾ cup) hot water

Cape gooseberry custard

500ml (2 cups) fresh cream
100ml (⅖ cup) milk
2ml (¼t) vanilla paste
4 egg yolks
80ml (⅓ cup) castor sugar
30ml (2T) cornflour (Maizena)
150g cape gooseberries, puréed

fresh cape gooseberries, quartered,
   to serve
sprigs of fresh mint, to serve

Serves 8

Malva pudding

1. Preheat the oven to 180°C.
2. Place the eggs and sugar in the bowl of a mixer and beat until thick and pale yellow.
3. Add the slightly cooled *Protea repens* syrup.
4. Sieve together the flour, bicarbonate of soda and salt.
5. In a small saucepan, melt the butter, then add the vinegar.
6. Alternately add the flour, melted butter and milk to the egg mixture, while beating slowly.
7. Once everything has been added, beat for a further 2 minutes on high speed.
8. Pour the mixture into a greased 20 x 26cm ovenproof dish, cover with a lid or foil and bake for 35–45 minutes.

Malva pudding sauce

1. Combine all the ingredients in a saucepan and heat gently until the sugar has dissolved. Set aside and keep warm.
2. As soon as the pudding comes out of the oven, pour over the warm sauce and leave for at least 15 minutes to soak up the syrup.

Cape gooseberry custard

1. Heat the cream, milk and vanilla paste in a saucepan.
2. In an electric mixer, beat the egg yolks, castor sugar and cornflour until well combined.
3. Slowly pour the warm cream mixture into the egg mixture, while whisking continuously.
4. Pour the custard into a clean pot and cook on a gentle heat until it starts to thicken (this should take 2–3 minutes).
5. Stir the puréed gooseberries into the custard, remove from the heat and set aside until needed. (Cover the custard with greaseproof paper or cling wrap to stop a skin forming.)

To serve

Cut the pudding into squares, pour over a little custard and garnish with fresh gooseberries and a sprig of fresh mint. Serve the rest of the custard on the side. The custard can be hot or cold, but the pudding should be warm, so if you make it ahead, reheat just before serving.

COOK'S NOTES

• You can substitute the *Protea repens* syrup (*see* page 143) with 15ml (1T) smooth apricot jam.
• Cape gooseberries (*Physalis*) get their name from the papery husk, or cape, that surrounds the small orange fruits.

WINE SUGGESTIONS

This relatively sweet dessert, with its hints of caramel, needs an equally full-bodied, spirity warmth to match it, so why not try an aged grape spirit.
• Cape Pot Still brandy (10 or 20 years old).
• Vintage Armagnac (at least 15 years old).

For Protea repens syrup, see page 143.

The Bot River Protea (*Protea compacta,* above) and Sugarbush Protea or Suikerbos (*Protea repens*, left) are two of the many *Protea* species that grow on the Estate.

Protea repens syrup

10 *Protea repens* flowers, well
  rinsed in cold water
500ml (2 cups) cold water
30ml (2T) Hamilton Russell
  Vineyards Fynbos Honey
100g white sugar

1. Add the cold water and honey to a large pot. Place the flowers, upside down, into the pot and boil for 25 minutes. Remove the flower heads and strain the syrup to remove any bits.
2. Return the strained syrup to a clean pot. Add 100g white sugar and boil for another 20 minutes until the syrup reaches thread stage. On a sugar thermometer, this would be between 108°C and 118°C (118° at sea level and one degree lower for every 300 metres above sea level).

COOK'S NOTES
*   This should make 100–120ml syrup. Store leftover syrup in a clean, sterilized glass jar.
*   Try to obtain protea flowers directly from the grower, and ask whether they have been sprayed with any pesticides. Most flowers sold in shops are unsuitable, as they will have been treated with chemicals to prolong their shelf life.

Winter

Lighting an evening fire
in the kitchen is one of
pleasures of winter.

RIGHT Eucalyptus (sugar gum) logs for the fire
come from our own forest.
FAR RIGHT Dormant vines ready for close pruning.

June

June is a time for rain and rest, firesides and friends. With the vines fully dormant and the annual vineyard cycle at an end, it is also a time for the vineyard team to rest. The cover crop between the vines thickens and lengthens, greening the land. Soaking rains from the northwest, having filled the water table, begin to fill the dams in earnest to overflowing. Drains and channels are cleared and repaired and the Estate's roads are protected from erosion. Farm equipment is overhauled in readiness for the season ahead and the coming year's vineyard plans are reviewed and embellished.

In the cellar, the Pinot Noir and Chardonnay brood and evolve in their small French oak barrels, in silence and in cold peace, only disturbed on occasion for comparative tastings. It's a time for tasting, quiet analysis, thinking and planning the next small refinements. The old climbing roses growing along the paddock fences and the beds of floribunda and 'Athene' roses at the cellar wear the last of their bravest flowers, along with their vivid red-orange rosehips.

The olive groves around the manor house steal a march on the vines and silver up with new growth, assisted by the rains. Free of their load after the harvest, they initiate the flowers that will become next season's olives. They look alive.

On the hill slopes, the Cape mountain fynbos is a blaze of lemon-yellow as the leucadendrons come to the fore, the white erica like a dusting of frost in between. The vivid pink *Protea compacta* punctuates the darker vegetation of the lower slopes and deeper sandstone soils. In the aloe garden, the flame-coloured flowers provide welcome sustenance for the shiny, emerald-green malachite sunbirds. The renosterveld flourishes on the clay-rich, shale-derived soils, in deep grey-greens, with the 'kooigoed' lending a beautiful, silvery brightness.

Winter is a quiet time for hosting our South African customers and friends for tastings in the barrel cellar and long lunches at home. It is the season to celebrate what has passed and plan for what will come. And on sunny days, harvesting glistening black mussels off the rocks in Hermanus is a perfect low-tide pursuit, either alone or with the children or friends.

*W*alker Bay black mussel bunny chow in a 'kooigoed' sauce

On cold winter weekends, it has become a bit of a family tradition to collect black mussels down at the coast and come home to enjoy them in front of a roaring fire. 'Bunny chow', which is basically a helping of curry served inside a hollowed-out loaf of bread, originated on the streets of Durban during the depression era. It derives its name from the 'bania', an Indian caste of merchants, who first served curry in this manner to African workers who were not allowed into cafés or diners at that time. This recipe is a more sophisticated version, using fresh mussels, coconut milk, and 'kooigoed', an indigenous shrub whose leaves impart a mild, curry-like flavour.

Mini-loaves

300g white bread flour
pinch of salt
10g (1 sachet) instant dry yeast
200–250ml (¾ –1 cup) lukewarm
    water
45ml (3T) finely grated lemon rind
10ml (2t) Hamilton Russell
    Vineyards Extra-virgin Olive Oil

Kooigoed sauce

8 green cardamom pods
90ml (6T) olive oil
2ml (¼t) cumin seeds
2ml (¼t) fennel seeds
2ml (¼t) coriander seeds
1ml (⅛t) mustard seeds
350g onions, finely chopped
2ml (¼t) ground turmeric
2ml (¼t) ground ginger
1ml (⅛ t) ground cinnamon
10ml (2t) cayenne pepper
60ml (4T) kooigoed leaves (*see*
    Cook's notes)
400ml (1¾ cups) coconut milk
400ml (1¾ cups) coconut cream
pinch of flaked salt

Mussels

1.5kg Walker Bay black mussels
    (*see* Cook's notes)
375ml (1½ cups) salted water
375ml (1½ cups) dry white wine
    (*see* Cook's notes)
45ml (3T) chopped fresh garlic

sprigs of fresh kooigoed, to serve

Serves 8

Mini-loaves

1. Sift the flour and salt together. Add the dry yeast, and mix.
2. Slowly add the water, while mixing with a wooden spoon. The mixture should not be too runny, so you may not need all the water.
3. Knead the mixture until it forms a firm ball (sprinkle over a little more flour if the dough is not firm enough).
4. Cover with a tea towel and leave to prove for 30 minutes, until the dough doubles in size.
5. Punch down the dough, while mixing in the lemon rind. Divide the dough into eight miniature loaf tins (± 4 x 5 x 9cm).
6. Leave to prove for another 15 minutes, then drizzle each loaf with a little olive oil.
7. Preheat the oven to 180°C and bake for 15–20 minutes, on the middle rack, until golden. Serve warm. These can be made the day before and reheated before serving.

Kooigoed sauce

1. Crush the cardamom pods with a pestle and mortar and remove the husks.
2. Heat the olive oil in a medium saucepan. Add the crushed cardamom, cumin, fennel, coriander and mustard seeds as well as the chopped onions.
3. Fry for about 3 minutes, until the onions become translucent.
4. Add the ground spices and the kooigoed leaves, and fry for a further 2 minutes.
5. Add the coconut milk and cream, turn the heat down and simmer for 10 minutes, while stirring occasionally. Add salt to taste.
The sauce can be made a few hours ahead and reheated before serving.

Mussels

1. Thoroughly scrub the mussels, removing any beards, and rinse well in cold, salted water. Discard any open mussels.
2. Put the mussels, salted water, wine and garlic into a large, heavy-based pot. Cover with a tight-fitting lid and steam over a high heat until the mussels open (about 3–5 minutes). Take care not to overcook them, as this will make the flesh rubbery. Discard any mussels that fail to open.
3. Drain the mussels in a colander (retain the garlic).
4. Wash and dry the pot. Pour the sauce into the pot, add the mussels and garlic and re-heat gently until just warmed through.

To serve

Halve the mini-loaves and hollow out the centres (serve these on the side). On each plate, arrange two halves of a loaf and spoon over the mussels and sauce. Top with a sprig of kooigoed.

COOK'S NOTES

- Ensure you have a permit to collect black mussels and stick to the daily limit. Mussels are harvested at low tide, so check the tide tables before you set out. Or opt for buying fresh or frozen mussels from a reputable supplier.
- For steaming the mussels, I use an older, nutty Chardonnay. For a variation, use a can of beer.
- Drying fresh kooigoed leaves for about a month before using intensifies their flavour. You can substitute dried curry leaves, using one leaf per 30ml (2T) dried kooigoed leaves.

WINE SUGGESTIONS

The creamy texture and full flavour of this dish needs a bold, crisp white wine, possibly with some age.
- Old vines Chenin Blanc from Riebeeck Kasteel or the Perdeberg region, Western Cape.
- Dry Pinot Gris from Alsace.
- Mosel Riesling (look for the eagle symbol of the VDP, a quality indicator, on the label or capsule).

Roasted Stellenbosch quails
with pancetta, black olive and honey stuffing

The richess of the quail meat is delightfully balanced by the very subtle hints of savoury and sweet in the stuffing. I like to serve these dainty birds with small Parisienne potatoes and extra-fine green beans, so as to not dwarf them.

Quails

150g (½ cup) table salt
60ml (4T) sugar
4 litres (16 cups) water
8 quails (*see* Cook's note)

Pancetta, black olive and honey stuffing

225g pancetta lardons (*see* Cook's notes)
185g breadcrumbs (± 6 slices of white bread, finely crumbled)
80g black kalamata-style olives, pitted and finely chopped
10g (½ cup) finely chopped flat-leaf parsley
30ml (2T) Hamilton Russell Vineyards Fynbos Honey, melted
90ml (6T) Hamilton Russell Vineyards Extra-virgin Olive Oil

To baste

90ml (6T) Hamilton Russell Vineyards Extra-virgin Olive Oil
45ml (3T) balsamic vinegar

Serves 8

Brining the quails

1. Dissolve the salt and sugar in cold water in a large airtight container.
2. Add the quails and refrigerate for 1–2 hours. (Don't leave the quails in the brine for longer, as they will be too salty.) Rinse under cold running water and pat dry.

Pancetta, black olive and honey stuffing

1. Fry the pancetta lardons over a high heat until crispy.
2. Remove the pan from the heat and add the breadcrumbs, tossing them in the pan juices.
3. Transfer the lardons and breadcrumbs to a bowl and add the olives, parsley, honey and olive oil, stirring well to combine. Set aside until cool.

Stuffing and roasting the quails

1. Preheat the oven to 200°C.
2. Divide the stuffing into 8 equal portions and stuff each quail body cavity.
3. Truss the birds using toothpicks (*see* Cook's note).
4. Place the quails, breast-side up, in an oiled roasting pan.
5. Combine the olive oil and balsamic vinegar, and brush a little over each quail.
6. Roast for 5 minutes at 200°C, reduce the heat to 150°C and roast for another 15–25 minutes, basting regularly. If the juices run clear when a skewer is pushed into the thigh, the quails are done. Leave to rest for 5 minutes, loosely covered with foil.

To serve

Pour over the pan juices and serve with Parisienne potatoes and Fresh green beans.

COOK'S NOTES

- Order deboned quails if possible; if they are frozen, defrost thoroughly in the fridge. Quails can dry out in the oven, but brining them beforehand helps the meat stay juicy and tender. Be careful not to overcook the quails, as this will cause them to lose flavour.
- If you can't get quails, use baby chickens (pouisson) instead, although the meat will not be as full-flavoured.
- To truss the stuffed quails, place them breast-side up and use your thumbs to tuck the wings between the legs and body, then bring the legs up and cross them. Use 2–3 toothpicks to secure the legs in this position.
- Lardons are pancetta off-cuts, cut into matchstick-thin strips. You can substitute very thinly cut strips of streaky bacon.
- If the olives are very salty, rinse them thoroughly beforehand.
- The easiest way to make fine breadcrumbs is in a food processor.

WINE SUGGESTIONS

A subtle classic, with flavours that require a savoury and firm red wine full of personality.

- Nebbiolo or Nebbiolo-blend from the Helderberg or Sir Lowry's Pass area of Somerset West, in the Western Cape.
- Barbaresco, a bold wine, made from the Nebbiolo grape, from Italy's Piedmont region.
- Aglianico del Vulture, a rich, chocolately wine from the Basilicata region of southern Italy

For Parisienne potatoes and Fresh green beans, see page 152.

Fresh green beans in a sesame dressing

Green beans

480g fine green beans, trimmed
45ml (3T) Hamilton Russell
Vineyards Extra-virgin Olive Oil

Sesame dressing

30ml (2T) sesame oil
45ml (3T) red wine vinegar
5ml (1t) soy sauce
2ml (¼t) Hamilton Russell
Vineyards Fynbos Honey, melted
1ml (⅛t) powdered ginger
10ml (2t) black sesame seeds

Green beans

1. In a large saucepan, bring 2 litres of lightly salted water to the boil.
2. Lightly blanch the beans until they turn bright green (3–4 minutes). Drain and pat dry.
3. Before serving, heat the olive oil in a wok or large frying pan and stir-fry the beans for 5 minutes.

Sesame dressing

1. Combine all the ingredients in a jug or small bowl.
2. Add to the cooked beans and toss lightly to coat. Serve immediately.

To serve

Serve with Roasted Stellenbosch quails, *see* page 151.

Parisienne potatoes with flat-leaf parsley

10–12 large potatoes, peeled
30g (2T) butter
3ml (½t) crushed fresh garlic
10ml (2t) finely chopped flat-leaf
parsley
15ml (1T) Hamilton Russell
Vineyards Extra-virgin Olive Oil

1. Using a melon baller, scoop rounded balls, about 3cm diameter, from the potatoes.
2. Bring a pot of water to the boil, and boil the potato balls for 5 minutes.
3. Drain in a colander, shaking gently to slightly roughen the surface.
4. Preheat the oven to 180°C.
5. Melt the butter in a roasting tray in the oven. When hot, add the potatoes, garlic and parsley, and drizzle with olive oil.
6. Roast for 25–30 minutes, until golden brown and crispy. Shake the roasting tray every 5–10 minutes to prevent the potatoes from sticking and to ensure they are well coated with the parsley, butter and oil.

To serve

Serve with Roasted Stellenbosch quails, *see* page 151.

COOK'S NOTES

*   Allow five Parisienne potatoes per person.
*   Use the leftover potato for soup or mash.

Milk tart in cinnamon phyllo pastry cases
with quince and rosehip cream

Milk tart or 'melktert' is a typically South African dessert, with Dutch origins. It has a higher milk to egg ratio than traditional custard, resulting in a light milk-flavoured tart. Milk tart is usually made as a large tart in a soft sweet pastry, but I love my creamier version, baked in individual crispy little cases. We collect quinces in mid-summer and bottle them in syrup, or make quince paste and jelly for use throughout the year. The reddish, berry-sized rosehips appear from late summer into early autumn, where spent flowers have been left on the rose bushes. It is easy to boil the rosehips into a fragrant syrup for use in sauces and cordials.

Phyllo pastry cases
235g butter, melted
70g castor sugar
20ml (4t) ground cinnamon
6 sheets phyllo pastry

Milk tart
375ml (1½ cups) full-cream milk
375ml (1½ cups) fresh cream
30g butter
2 eggs, separated
200g castor sugar
30ml (2T) cornflour (Maizena), sifted
60ml (4T) cake flour, sifted
7.5ml (1½t) vanilla paste or extract
pinch of salt

Quince and rosehip cream
500ml (2 cups) fresh cream
220g quince paste (*see* page 156)
60ml (4T) rosehip syrup (*see* page 156)
20ml (4t) fresh lemon juice

ground cinnamon, to serve
fresh lavender flowers, to serve

Serves 8

Phyllo pastry cases
1. Preheat the oven to 180°C.
2. Lightly spray eight ramekins (± 9cm diameter) with a non-stick vegetable spray.
3. Combine the sugar and ground cinnamon.
4. Cut each phyllo pastry sheet into four, so you have 24 smaller squares. Keep covered with a damp cloth to prevent the pastry from drying out.
5. Brush the first square with melted butter and sprinkle with cinnamon sugar. Place another square on top, brush with butter and sugar. Repeat with a third square, but do not brush with butter or sprinkle with sugar.
6. Drape the squares over an upside down panna cotta mould or small tumbler, and gently press down with a ramekin to form a cup-like case. You can also layer the phyllo squares in a muffin or cupcake pan.
7. Trim the pastry edges, then remove the panna cotta mould, leaving the phyllo case in the ramekin. Repeat until you have eight cases.
8. Brush the edges and inside of the cases with melted butter and bake for about 20 minutes, until crispy and golden. If the base of the cooked case is not even, press it down gently with a panna cotta mould or small tumbler to flatten it. Once cooled, remove the phyllo pastry cases from the ramekins and store in an airtight container until required.

Milk tart
1. In a medium saucepan, scald the milk and cream just until bubbles start to appear, then add the butter. Remove from the heat once the butter has melted, and set aside.
2. In a clean bowl, use an electric beater to whisk together the egg yolk and sugar until pale yellow. Add the sifted cornflour, cake flour and vanilla paste and fold in gently.

3. Add the warm milk and cream mixture to the egg mixture. Whisk gently to combine, pour back into the pot and return to a low heat.
4. Using a wire whisk, whisk continuously over a low heat for 10 minutes, until the mixture becomes thick and glossy.
5. Transfer to a clean metal bowl and set aside for 15 minutes to cool.
6. In a clean bowl, add a pinch of salt to the egg whites. Whisk until glossy stiff peaks form.
7. Using a wire whisk, gently fold the egg whites into the cooled custard.
8. Spoon the custard into the phyllo pastry cases. Leave to set for at least 30 minutes (no longer than 1½ hours or the pastry will get soggy).

Quince and rosehip cream
1. In a saucepan, bring the cream to the boil and simmer for 2 minutes.
2. Add the quince paste, rosehip syrup and lemon juice and simmer for about 20 minutes, stirring regularly, until the cream has been reduced by one-quarter and is thick enough to coat the back of a spoon. Set aside to cool.

To serve
Sprinkle each milk tart with a little ground cinnamon, top with a fresh lavender flower and serve with the quince and rosehip cream.

WINE SUGGESTIONS
The creamy texture and subtle floral notes of this dessert require an aromatic wine, ideally with bubbles.
- South African dry (brut) sparkling wine.
- Prosecco, Italy's flagship sparkling wine, offers hints of green apples and gentle floral notes.
- Clairette de Die, a fresh, elegant sparkling wine from France's Rhône Valley.

For Quince paste and Rosehip syrup, see page 156.

Quince paste

This paste can also be served with roast pork or venison, or as part of a cheese platter, with other preserves. Quinces are in season in summer, but bottled quince jelly is available all year round.

2–3 ripe quinces, peeled, cored
    and quartered
castor sugar

Makes about 200g

1. Preheat the oven to 150°C.
2. Put the quince quarters into an ovenproof dish and bake, covered, for about an hour, until the fruit is soft but not breaking up.
3. Purée the cooked quinces in an electric blender. Weigh the purée.
4. Put the weighed purée into a heavy based pot and add the same amount of castor sugar. Simmer for 20–30 minutes, stirring continuously until the paste starts to pull away from the edges of the pot.
5. Line a baking tray with greaseproof paper and pour over the paste, spreading it 2–3cm deep. Smooth the surface and leave for about 3 hours, until set. Store in the fridge.

Rosehip syrup

100g rosehips
75ml (5T) castor sugar
45ml (3T) Hamilton Russell
    Vineyards Fynbos Honey

1. Remove the stalks from the rosehips and place the hips in a small non-stick or stainless steel pan. Add the castor sugar and honey, and just cover with water.
2. Bring to the boil and simmer gently until the rosehips are soft (this could take 1–2 hours, depending on how large and firm they are). Stir occasionally and top up with a dash of boiling water if necessary. After about 40 minutes, start mashing the rosehips gently with a potato masher.
3. Strain the soft-cooked fruit through a fine sieve, pressing down with a wooden spoon to extract as much syrup as possible (discard the pulp). Store the syrup in a clean, airtight jar or container.

COOK'S NOTES
- Rosehips appear at the end of the rose flowering season; just leave the spent flowers on the bush, don't prune them off.
- If you want to harvest rosehips, it is important that you do not spray your roses with any form of pesticide or insectide shortly before harvesting. Consult your nursery or garden centre for advice on products suitable for use on edible plants.

Winter's cool, crisp days are perfect for harvesting black mussels off the rocks.

LEFT Quince trees are a regular feature of many old Cape farms.

RIGHT Gathering nori seaweed from the rock pools of Walker Bay.

LEFT 'Kooigoed' (*Helichrysum* spp.) is a small sliver-grey everlasting shrub with aromatic leaves that impart a mild curry-like flavour. It is indigenous to the Cape and, on Hamilton Russell Vineyards, thrives on the clay-rich soils of the Renosterveld. RIGHT Harvesting black mussels off the rocks at low tide; seafood doesn't come fresher than this.

ABOVE AND RIGHT On many winter mornings, the mist hangs low over the Hemel-en-Aarde Valley.

Strong northwesters and cold fronts alternate with cool, bright wind-free days with scarcely a cloud in the sky.

July

The rains and the cold nights and days continue, as do the periodic northwesterly fronts that sweep in from the stormy Atlantic. But, from time to time, we are blessed with cool, bright, wind-free days with scarcely a cloud in the sky. On many mornings, mist hangs low over the Hemel-en-Aarde Valley, until the sun emerges from behind the ancient, folded sandstone mountains and burns it off. If you are lucky, with a gentle southeasterly breeze at dusk, you can hear the muffled bass roar of the Atlantic meeting the Hermanus coastline two kilometres to the South; even smell the heady mix of kelp and brine. It is clean sea and a big sea.

Recharged after their midyear holidays, the vineyard team tackles the winter pruning with enthusiasm, their secateurs clicking like out of season crickets as they work their way down the rows. The cuts made now have a bearing on harvest size and quality and they proceed with care. Pruning is half art, half craft and their experience is valuable. In the new vineyard blocks, poles are planted in perfect rows in preparation for August planting. Soil profiles are dug and samples sent away for analysis. Soil can only be properly prepared once in the life of a vineyard, so great care is taken to plan it well.

In the cellar, the winemaking team carefully tops up the barrels fortnightly, to compensate for the tiny amount of desirable evaporation which is controlled by the grain of the oak, and the temperature and humidity of the cellar. They check the Chardonnay barrels for the progress of malolactic fermentation, and the Pinot Noir barrels for any problems with the health of the lees that may require racking.

The mountain fynbos is still wearing its winter yellows. The occasional sticky *Protea repens* shows its glazed ivory head above shaggy, dark-stemmed bushes. *Protea longifolia* offers up its woolly core of seeds to the elements, while the shell-pink *Protea compacta* continues to bud and thrive. The Cape sugarbirds are grateful. In the wetlands the arums are at their best and the snowdrops flourish under old oaks and where there were once, perhaps, walls and gardeners.

More friends come to stay over weekends and there are kitchen suppers by a hot fire of eucalyptus logs and afternoon walks in the fynbos.

Smoked snoek chowder with wild sorrel
served with lemon thyme mini-loaves

Snoek is a quintessentially Cape fish. In fact, it is to Cape fishing villages what cod is to Portugal. This barracuda-like fish is traditionally caught on a hand-line from small fishing boats and sold directly from the boats or from the back of vehicles in harbours and alongside the road. Snoek is a seasonal catch, so fresh snoek is often an opportunistic find. This fish has a very short 'shelf life', and most snoek that is sold fresh off the boats is bought for braaiing the same day. Snoek that is not destined to be sold quickly is usually smoked, or turned into pâtés or terrines. Unless you live right at the coast, you will have to rely on smoked snoek. This often-dry fish lends itself to the moisturising, flavour-moderating influence of a soup and I find that its intrinsically rich flavours complement a chowder-like soup.

Smoked snoek chowder

750ml (3 cups) fresh cream
250g smoked snoek, skinned, deboned and flaked
40g (3T) butter
45ml (3T) Hamilton Russell Vineyards Extra-virgin Olive Oil
90g leeks, finely chopped
1 medium onion, finely chopped
12 cloves garlic, finely chopped
70g (½ cup) flour
750ml (3 cups) milk
160ml (⅔ cup) gherkins, chopped
5ml (1t) lemon rind, finely grated
80ml (⅓ cup) Hamilton Russell Vineyards Chardonnay (*see* Cook's notes)
10ml (2t) fresh lemon juice
150g extra flaked smoked snoek, for serving
20g wild sorrel, finely shredded (*see* Cook's notes)

Lemon thyme mini-loaves

300g white bread flour
pinch of salt
10g (1 sachet) instant yeast
200–250ml (¾–1 cup) lukewarm water
30ml (2T) lemon thyme leaves
15ml (1T) Hamilton Russell Vineyards Extra-virgin Olive Oil

Wasabi cream

35ml (2½T) fresh cream
5ml (1t) wasabi powder
salt and pepper, to taste

Serves 8

Smoked snoek chowder

1. In a small saucepan, heat the cream until small bubbles appear on the surface.
2. Add the flaked, smoked snoek and simmer over low heat for 20 minutes. Set aside, covered, for at least 30 minutes to allow the flavours to infuse.
3. In a separate, larger pot, melt the butter, add the olive oil and heat, then add the leeks, onion and garlic and fry until the onions become translucent. Reduce the heat slightly, if necessary, as you don't want the onions to brown.
4. Stir in the flour, and cook for one minute.
5. Add the milk very slowly, whisking constantly with a wire whisk to prevent lumps from forming.
6. Add the gherkins, lemon rind and wine.
7. Strain the snoek-infused cream and add to the soup. Discard the fish.
8. Reheat gently just before serving, adding the lemon juice, extra smoked snoek and the sorrel. Stir gently to combine.

Lemon thyme mini-loaves

1. Preheat the oven to 180°C.
2. Sift the flour and salt together. Add the yeast and combine.
3. Slowly add the water while mixing with a wooden spoon. The mixture should not be too runny, so you may not need all the water.
4. Turn out onto a clean board and knead the dough until it forms a firm ball (sprinkle over a little more flour if it is not firm enough).
5. Cover with a tea towel and leave to prove for 30 minutes, or until the dough doubles in size.
6. Punch down the dough, while mixing in the lemon thyme leaves.
7. Divide the dough into eight mini-loaf tins (± 4 x 5 x 9cm). Leave to prove for 15 minutes, then drizzle with olive oil and bake for 15–20 minutes, on the middle rack, until golden.

Wasabi cream

Combine the cream and wasabi powder in a small bowl or jug. Season to taste.

To serve

Top each bowl of chowder with a teaspoon of wasabi cream and serve, accompanied by the mini-loaves.

COOK'S NOTES

- Both wild and garden sorrel are in season in winter. If you can't get sorrel, substitute with baby spinach or English spinach and increase the lemon juice in the soup to 15ml (3t).
- I prefer to use a young, wooded Chardonnay in the soup, as it will have some richness with a nice balance of acidity.
- Make sure you remove all the bones from the fish.
- If you can't get snoek, use a full-flavoured smoked fish, such as mackerel or haddock.
- The mini-loaves can be made the day before and reheated before serving.

WINE SUGGESTIONS

Smoked snoek has considerable flavour and texture, and this soup has the added zing of wasabi-flavoured cream. It needs a juicy, stony, oily wine with a subtle oak influence to stand up to it.

- Rousannne from Stellenbosch. This white variety, from France's Rhône Valley, offers notes of pears, apples, nuts and toffee.
- Gaillac, an elegant, complex white wine with hints of orange peel, quince and hay, that comes from southwestern France.
- Crozes-Hermitage, a richly textured, complex white wine from the Rhône, incorporating both Marsanne and Rousanne grapes, which give it juicy acidity and notes of spice and pear.

In July, as if to compensate for the cold, the mountain fynbos wears its winter yellows.

LEFT Colin leads his vineyard team as they tackle the winter pruning.

RIGHT The tickberry or 'bosluisbessie', commonly known as 'bietou', flowers from late summer to midwinter.

LEFT Entertaining continues all year round, as we welcome guests to our home.

RIGHT In winter, *Leucadendrons* (cone flowers) add colour to the hillsides.

$\mathcal{P}$an-fried fillet of beef
with a creamy horseradish sauce

It is no secret that South African beef ranks amongst the best in the world. For many people, lean, tender fillet is the best of beef. Cook the fillet medium-rare and serve it hot, accompanied by rosemary-skewered roast potatoes and a colourful warm salad.

1.6kg beef fillet, trimmed

Marinade
60ml (4T) Hamilton Russell
  Vineyards Extra-virgin Olive Oil
15ml (1T) dark soy sauce
15ml (1T) fresh lemon juice
15ml (1T) pink verjuice (*see*
  Cook's notes)
15ml (1T) chopped fresh rosemary
  leaves
3ml (½t) finely grated lemon rind

Creamy horseradish sauce
500ml (2 cups) fresh cream
75ml (5T) grated fresh horseradish
15ml (1T) hot English mustard

Serves 8

Marinade
1. Combine all the marinade ingredients. Place the fillet in a non-metallic dish, rub over the marinade and leave for at least 1 hour.
2. Heat a cast-iron griddle pan and sear the fillet on all sides to seal (the griddle marks should be very dark brown). Remove the fillet from the griddle pan.
3. Preheat the oven to 180°C.
4. Put the marinated fillet into a roasting pan or ovenproof dish. Place on the middle rack and cook for 10 minutes, then turn off the oven and leave for another 5 minutes.
5. Remove the fillet from the oven and leave to rest for at least 10 minutes. Slice into 8 steaks (±2cm thick) and serve accompanied by the sauce.

Creamy horseradish sauce
1. In a small saucepan, scald the cream (heat to just below boiling).
2. Add the fresh horseradish and mustard and stir to combine.
3. Reduce the heat to low and simmer for 20 minutes, stirring occasionally.
   Serve immediately, or cover until needed, then reheat gently.

COOK'S NOTES
- The fillet can be marinated and seared up to eight hours in advance and set aside, covered, until ready to serve. Bring to room temperature before roasting.
- If you can't get fresh horseradish, use 60ml (4T) prepared creamed or pickled horseradish.
- Make the sauce close to serving, as it will separate if left to stand for more than an hour or two.
- Verjuice is extracted from unripened grapes. It is naturally mildly acidic and can be used in cooking, as a condiment or to deglaze pans. Pink verjuice is made from unripe red grapes. You can use either normal verjuice or pink verjuice for this dish.

WINE SUGGESTIONS
A delicate, structured red with some bottle ageing will be a fine match.
- Barbera, with its dark fruit and toasty oak aromas, from Durbanville in the Western Cape.
- Pinotage blend from the cool-climate Walker Bay district.
- For a special occasion, choose a Bordeaux; a third growth Margaux, at least five years old, will be sublime.

For Warm salad of multi-coloured chard, see page 168; and Rosemary-skewered roast potatoes, see page 169.

Warm salad of multi-coloured chard and red onion

Chard and spinach are rich in micronutrients and phytonutrients, and the multi-coloured stalks provide additional antioxidant activity. Red onions have a lovely mild, sweet flavour which works beautifully with chard.

4 large red onions, peeled
10ml (2t) dark soy sauce
10ml (2t) Hamilton Russell
    Vineyards Extra-virgin Olive Oil
1 litre (4 cups) chicken stock
600g multi-coloured chard,
    washed and trimmed
40g butter
60ml (4T) pink verjuice (*see*
    Cook's notes)
20g finely grated mature Klein
    River Gruyére Cheese

1. Preheat the oven to 120°C. Cut two of the onions into quarters. Place on a baking tray, drizzle with soy sauce and olive oil and roast for 25 minutes, moving the onions around every 10–15 minutes to stop them from sticking. Set aside until required.
2. In a medium saucepan, bring the chicken stock to the boil. Chop the remaining two onions finely, add them to the stock and cook for 5 minutes.
3. Roughly chop the chard (leaves and stems) and add to the chicken stock. Cook for a further 2 minutes. Drain, reserving the stock.
4. Transfer the blanched chard and onions to a serving bowl. Mix in the roasted onion quarters.
5. In a small bowl, whisk the butter and verjuice into 125ml warm chicken stock and drizzle over the spinach and onions. Sprinkle over the Gruyére cheese and serve immediately.

COOK'S NOTES
- Each onion should weigh about 130g. Use extra onions, if necessary.
- Red onions are also known as sweet Italian onions, Italian red onions, Creole onions and red torpedo onions.
- Multi-coloured chard is called Swiss chard, silverbeet, perpetual spinach, spinach beet, crab beet or bright lights. If you can't get multi-coloured chard, you can substitute any of the spinach varieties.
- A full-flavoured Gruyére (12 months matured) is best, but you could also use a good-quality Parmigano Reggiano or Grana Padano.

Rosemary-skewered roast potatoes

48 baby potatoes, scrubbed
60ml (4T) Hamilton Russell Vineyards Extra-virgin Olive Oil
16 rosemary twigs, each about 25cm long
15ml (1T) flaked salt

1. Preheat the oven to 180°C. Place the potatoes on a large baking tray
    and drizzle over the olive oil, turning the potatoes until they are coated
    on all sides. Roast for 40 minutes, shaking the tray every 10–15 minutes to
    prevent the potatoes from sticking to the tray.
2. Turn up the heat to 200°C and roast for another 10 minutes.
3. Carefully rinse and dry the rosemary twigs and strip the leaves off the
    bottom 20cm of each twig. As soon as the potatoes are cooked, skewer three
    potatoes onto each rosemary twig. Sprinkle with salt and serve immediately.

COOK'S NOTES
*   Allow two potato skewers per person.
*   Only skewer the potatoes onto the twigs just before serving, as heat will
    brown the rosemary.

Hamilton Russell Vineyards Pinot Noir-poached pear brûlée tart

One of the earliest references to pears is found in Homer's Odyssey, where pears are called 'a gift of the gods'. With its warm sweet flavours, this tart is the kitchen's winter gift to the home. The filling is an adaptation of a war-time recipe discovered in the family holiday house by my mother-in-law in the early 1960s.

Pinot Noir-poached pears

400g fresh pears, peeled, halved and cored
  (*see* Cook's notes)
500ml (2 cups) Hamilton Russell Vineyards
  Pinot Noir, current vintage
60ml (4T) castor sugar
5ml (1t) fresh lemon juice
5 cloves
3ml (½t) ground cinnamon

Sweet pastry

75g icing sugar
1 star anise, ground (*see* Cook's notes)
120g butter
2 egg yolks
250g cake flour, sifted

Custard filling

160g butter
140g (1 cup) cake flour, sifted
750ml (3 cups) milk
260g (1¼ cups) castor sugar
6 egg yolks
60ml (4T) cornflour (Maizena)
5ml (1t) vanilla paste

Pear and pomegranate sauce

poaching liquid from the pears, strained
125ml (½ cup) unsweetened pomegranate juice
15g (2T) dried pomegranate arils (pips)

castor sugar, to serve
fresh mint leaves, for garnish

Serves 8

Pinot Noir-poached pears

1. Slice each pear half lengthwise into three and set aside.
2. Place all the other ingredients into a medium saucepan and warm, while stirring gently.
3. Once the sugar has dissolved, add the pear slices, reduce the heat and simmer for 18–20 minutes, ensuring the pears do not get too soft to handle.
4. Remove the saucepan from the heat and leave to cool. Once cooled, transfer the pears and the poaching liquid to an airtight container. Store in the fridge for at least 5 hours, but preferably overnight.

Sweet pastry

1. Combine the icing sugar and ground star anise.
2. In a food processor or mixer, cream the butter and flavoured icing sugar.
3. Add the egg yolks, one by one, and mix until smooth and creamy.
4. Add all the flour at once, and mix just until it comes together.
5. Transfer the pastry to a sheet of cling wrap, shape into a ball, wrap and place in the fridge to rest for 30 minutes.
6. Spray a 26cm loose-based tart tin with non-stick cooking spray.
7. Sprinkle some icing sugar on a clean work surface. Unwrap the chilled pastry, flatten slightly and roll out to a diameter of 18–20cm.
8. Lift the pastry onto the rolling pin and unroll it into the tin. Press the pastry evenly into the base and sides of the tin, making sure it is no thicker than 2mm. Trim the edges, cover with cling wrap and rest in the fridge for 15 minutes.
9. Preheat the oven to 150°C
10. Remove the pastry case from the fridge, uncover and prick the base with a fork. Line the pastry case with baking paper (making sure the sides are covered), fill with baking beans and blind bake for 30 minutes. Set aside to cool.

Custard filling

1. Melt the butter in a saucepan. Once melted, slowly add the flour, using a wire whisk to mix it into the butter. The mixture will form a ball. Lower the heat to medium and continue stirring for about 2 minutes.
2. Start adding the milk very slowly, ensuring that each addition of milk is smoothly blended in before adding more. Remove from the heat.
3. In a separate bowl, whisk together the castor sugar, egg yolks, cornflour and vanilla paste until the egg yolks turn pale yellow.
4. Add the milk mixture to the egg mixture. Combine well, return to a medium heat and whisk continuously for 10 minutes, until it thickens.
5. Spoon the custard into the cooled pastry case and smooth over.

Pear and pomegranate sauce

1. Drain the pear slices, retaining the poaching liquid. Discard the cloves and cinnamon and set the pears aside.
2. Transfer the poaching liquid to a small pot and place over a medium heat. Add the pomegranate juice and arils and heat gently, stirring regularly, until reduced by half. Keep warm.

Assembling and serving the tart

It is best to assemble the tart while the custard filling is still warm.

1. Arrange the poached pear slices in a circular pattern on top of the filling and set aside at room temperature to cool.
2. Just before serving, sprinkle 75ml (5T) castor sugar evenly over the tart. Using a hand-held gas burner, caramelize the sugar to a crisp, golden brûlée crust.
3. Cut into individual slices, drizzle over some sauce, garnish with fresh mint leaves and serve immediately. Serve any remaining sauce on the side.

COOK'S NOTES

- I like to use Forelle pears, as they remain fairly firm even when ripe.
- Grind the star anise to a very fine powder. A stone pestle and mortar works well.
- Poach the pears up to two days ahead and store, covered, in the fridge. Do not discard the poaching liquid, as it is used to make the sauce.
- Make the pastry base up to a day in advance, but only add the filling a couple of hours before serving, so the pastry remains crunchy. If made in advance, wrap the base in cling wrap and store in the fridge.
- If the filling gets a touch lumpy, use a hand-held blender to smooth it out.
- When caramelizing the castor sugar for the brûlée crust, hold the burner 25–30cm from the tart.
- If you can't get pomegranate juice, substitute with unsweetened pure cranberry juice, like the Ocean Spray brand (use pure juice, not a blend).

WINE SUGGESTIONS

Be daring with the wine, or opt for a spirit-based fruit brandy (eau de vie) instead.

- Pinot Noir from the Hemel-en-Aarde Valley; choose the current release and serve slightly chilled.
- Pinot Noir Ice Wine from Canada's Okanagan Valley.
- Chilled Poire William or Framboise eau de vie.

This willow tree looks bare now, but in Spring it comes alive as the Weavers colonize it.

RIGHT One of the older Pinot Noir vineyards on the slope behind the Estate's first olive grove.

August

The windy month. Sometimes we get off lightly, sometimes we don't. Olive trees whip around in the howling northwest wind, shutters rattle and driving rain sounds like sand thrown on the windowpanes. An extra log or two is placed on the fire. Everything outside seems angry and it is a time to be indoors. But Nature can't be angry for long and the cold fronts pass. A cool, still sunny morning and a large flock of guineafowl pick their way slowly across wet grass, feeding opportunistically. Gorgeous dark grey-blue, yellow-billed rameron pigeons are surprised feeding in the trees on left-over olives, while a solitary fiscal shrike, staking his annual claim to a large *Aloe bainsii*, flamboyantly advertises his abundant territory to a prospective partner. There is at least a belief in Spring – a strong one judging from the profusion of deeply scented violets.

In the vineyards the last of the pruning continues. Heads are down and hands are purposeful. The big sleep won't last much longer. The pink oxalis are beginning to show, like wedding confetti, on the cellar lawns. Organic fertilizer is ordered and the data from soil sampling is analysed for any small adjustments which may be required. Workers who are not pruning are carefully planting out the new vines; holes are dug with a fork to avoid any smearing of the damp clay, and a large scoop of mushroom compost gets the vines off to a good start. Their wine will be tasted for the first time in four years, an expression of the essence of place.

The passive side of winemaking is underway, with all wines slowly evolving in the barrel. The last of the malolactic fermentations finish in the cool, humid cellar. The Chardonnay undergoes two more rounds of *batonnage*, a gentle stirring of the lees back into suspension to add complexity and body to the wine.

It's a time to collect stone pine cones with the children. The delicious resinous, aromatic nuts may be difficult to get at, but a hard-earned pesto or tapenade is the best-tasting. Around the stone pines and along the wetland, invasive *Acacia longifolia* that escaped the last clearing are in full, sweet, honey-scented flower. There's excitement in the fynbos reserve. *Sonderothamnus speciosus* is in flower; all eight plants! It is endangered and extremely rare, with only a few dozen known plants in the mountains around Hermanus. The hillside roses up as the pink erica, or heath, comes into full flower alongside the white. On the middle slopes, bright red-headed, white-bearded pagoda bushes (*Mimetes* spp.) look like misplaced garden gnomes, while on the wetter, deep soils of the lower slopes, the cream-ball topped *Brunia*, with their feathery lime-green foliage, sharpen up the landscape.

August is a quiet month, but the sap is rising and the year is gathering speed.

Waterblommetjie risotto with bokkoms

Waterblommetjies, the flowers of *Aponogeton distachyos*, are common in dams and ponds throughout the Western Cape. The edible flowers and buds are ready to be picked in late winter, so August is a good time to enjoy them. They are traditionally cooked with beef or mutton in a tasty stew or 'bredie'. It is likely that waterblommetjies ('small water flowers') were used as a food source by the indigenous Khoikhoi, and adopted by the early Dutch settlers at the Cape, who used them as a vegetable and a valuable source of vitamin C. The Voortrekkers are believed to have harvested waterblommetjies during the Great Trek.

In many West Coast fishing villages, rows of small fish strung on rope can be seen drying in the wind under reed shelters. These are harders, or mullet, which are caught by the local fishermen. Once salted and air-dried they are known as 'bokkoms', and form part of the culinary heritage of this region.

1.5 litres (6 cups) chicken stock
500g waterblommetjies, washed and trimmed
30ml (2T) Hamilton Russell Vineyards Extra-virgin Olive Oil
30g (2T) butter
½ red onion, finely chopped
1–2 cloves garlic, finely chopped
500g risotto rice
60ml (4T) Hamilton Russell Vineyards Chardonnay
60ml (¼ cup) finely grated mature Klein River Gruyére Cheese
45ml (3T) fresh cream
5ml (1t) powdered bokkoms (*see* Cook's notes)

grated Gruyére cheese, to serve
Hamilton Russell Vineyards Extra-virgin Olive Oil, to serve

Serves 8

1. Bring one litre of chicken stock to the boil in a medium-sized pot. Add the waterblommetjies and cook for about 35 minutes, until tender. Strain, retaining the stock. You should have about 500ml stock left. Top it up to 700ml with the remaining chicken stock.
2. Purée 150g (± 1 cup) of cooked waterblommetjies. Set the rest of the waterblommetjies aside. Add the puréed waterblommetjies to the stock and keep warm.
3. In a large pot, heat the olive oil and butter. Add the onion and garlic and fry for about 4 minutes, until the onion becomes glossy and translucent. Add the risotto rice and fry until the grains are well coated in the buttery sauce, about 1 minute.
4. Pour in the wine and stir gently. Turn the heat down to a simmer. As soon as the wine has been absorbed by the rice, add a ladle-full of hot stock. When the stock has been absorbed, add another ladle-full, and repeat until all the stock has been absorbed. Stir gently to ensure that the rice does not burn, but don't overdo it, or the rice will become porridge-like. It's important to keep the heat very low.
5. Pick out eight whole waterblommetjies. Add the remainder to the risotto, plus the Gruyére cheese and the cream and give it a final stir to combine.

To serve
Serve in individual bowls, topped with a waterblommetjie and a sprinkling of powdered bokkoms. Place additional grated Gruyére cheese and olive oil on the table for guests to add their own.

COOK'S NOTES
- For a vegetarian version, substitute the chicken stock with vegetable stock.
- You can use any decent unwooded Chardonnay for the risotto.
- To make the risotto ahead of time, remove the pot from the heat when about two ladles of stock are left. Add the remaining stock, together with the whole waterblommetjies, Gruyére cheese and cream, and set aside covered until needed, then reheat gently and serve.
- Waterblommetjies can be substituted with fresh green asparagus tips. Use the stems and some tips to make the stock, retaining two to three tips per portion as a garnish.
- To make bokkom powder, use a large knife to chop the bokkoms to a fine powder. Bokkoms are very strongly flavoured and, for this recipe, you only need a small amount. As an alternative, finely chop three or four anchovy fillets and pan-fry them until crispy.

WINE SUGGESTIONS
This is a challenging dish when it comes to wine pairing. Either go for an aromatic white wine with some residual sugar to stand up to the salty tang of the bokkoms and mature Gruyére, or opt for a linear, minerally dry white.
- Bukettraube, an off-dry wine with honey and spice notes, from the Cedarberg, Western Cape.
- Dry Muscat, from Alsace in northeastern France, offers musky, exotic aromas and a delicate lemony taste.
- Jurançon Sec or Pacherenc du Vic-Bilh, from southwestern France, combine Semillon and Sauvignon Blanc with regional varieties to produce wines with aromas of peach, pineapple and almonds, and lemony acidity.

Although we receive fewer visitors in August, there is still plenty to do in the kitchen.

LEFT Pale green, nymph-like waterblommetjies (*Aponogeton distachyos*) emerge on the ponds at this time of year.

RIGHT Lending a helping hand, Olive's sister, Christine, selects a decanter for the Pinot Noir.

LEFT One of a collection of pestles and mortars is put to use crushing spices.

RIGHT Cool hands are needed when making a pastry case for a sweet tart.

Breast of guinea fowl
with olive and rosemary tapenade

Guinea fowl are a South African icon. These hardy game birds thrive in the veld but are becoming increasingly common in urban areas. Although they are domesticated in Europe, suprisingly, this is not a widespread practise in South Africa, and guinea fowl breasts might be difficult to obtain. The hearty flavour of guinea fowl is nicely complemented by this versatile tapenade, made from black olives, anchovies and capers. I took inspiration from another Mediterranean classic, pesto, and included pine nuts.

Guinea fowl

8 breasts of guinea fowl, deboned
   and skinned (*see* Cook's notes)
60ml (4T) Hamilton Russell
   Vineyards Extra-virgin Olive Oil
30ml (2T) balsamic vinegar
3ml (½t) Hamilton Russell
   Vineyards Fynbos Honey, melted
caperberries, for serving

Olive and rosemary tapenade

300g stoned black olives
3ml (½t) fresh rosemary leaves,
   chopped
3–4 anchovy fillets, chopped
15ml (1T) chopped capers
5ml (1t) freshly crushed garlic
15ml (1T) pine nuts
30ml (2T) Hamilton Russell
   Vineyards Extra-virgin Olive Oil
10ml (2t) fresh lemon juice
freshly ground black pepper, to
   taste

caperberries, to serve

Serves 8

Guinea fowl

1. Preheat the oven to 180°C.
2. Place the guinea fowl breasts in an ovenproof dish. Mix together the olive oil, balsamic vinegar and melted honey, and drizzle over the breasts. Cover the dish with a lid or foil and bake for 20 minutes.
3. Make 1½ cm-deep cuts into each breast, taking care not to cut all the way through. Using a hand-held blowtorch, brown each breast. Serve immediately.

Olive and rosemary tapenade

1. Combine all the ingredients in a blender and mix to a coarse paste. Season to taste.
2. Scoop into a bowl and keep cool until required.

To serve

Slice each guinea fowl breast and serve with Turnip and parsnip pureé (*see* page 182). Top with a few caperberries and pass around the tapenade for guests to help themselves.

COOK'S NOTES

*   If you can't obtain guinea fowl, use chicken breasts, although the flavour will not be as rich.
*   The tapenade can be made a day or two ahead and stored in a sealed container in the fridge.
*   If you don't have a blowtorch, put the breasts under a hot grill for a minute or two to brown, but take care not to burn them.

WINE SUGGESTIONS

A light to medium-bodied, elegant and aromatic red wine with some bottle age will be perfect to enhance the robust flavours of this dish.

*   Pinot Noir from the Hemel-en-Aarde Valley, with at least four years' age.
*   Volnay Premier Cru, a delicate red with a cherry scent, from Burgundy's Côte de Beaune. Seek out wines that are at least six years' old.
*   Quality Beaujolais Cru, such as Juliénas or Moulin-à-Vent, with hints of violets and blackcurrants, offer more structure than most early-drinking Gamay-based Beaujolais wines, meaning they last longer, too.

Turnip and parsnip purée

800g turnips, peeled and diced
1kg parsnips, peeled and diced
pinch of flaked salt
15ml (1T) Hamilton Russell
  Vineyards Extra-virgin Olive Oil

Violet-flower water

16 fresh violet flowers, rinsed (*see*
  Cook's notes)
30ml (2T) boiling water

fresh rosemary or violet flowers,
  to garnish

Serves 8

1. Boil the turnips and parsnips in lightly salted water until tender.
2. Drain well, removing all excess water.
3. Put the vegetables into a blender or food processor, add salt and olive oil and blend until smooth.
4. Set aside, covered, until required and reheat just before serving.

Violet-flower water

1. Pull the petals off 16 violet flowers and put them into a cup or small bowl with the boiling water.
2. Use a teaspoon to crush the violet petals to extract as much colour as possible.

To serve

Pipe or spoon the purée onto plate and drizzle over some violet-flower water. Garnish with a few fresh rosemary or violet flowers.

COOK'S NOTES

- *Viola odorata* (English violet) is native to Europe and Asia and introduced in North America and Australasia. It is also known as sweet violet, common violet or garden violet. The sweet scent was particularly popular in the late Victorian period, and has been used in many cosmetic fragrances and perfumes. The French are known for their violet syrup, which is made from an extract of violets. In the USA, French violet syrup is used to make violet scones and marshmallows. The species that is best known in South Africa is *Viola cornuta* (Johnny jump-up), a small, perennial plant with purple flowers with yellow, white and blue highlights. *V. cornuta* flowers are edible.
- If you want to pick edible flowers from your garden, do not use toxic insecticides or pesticides on your plants. Never consume flowers purchased for the vase, as they may have been treated before or after picking to prolong their shelf life.

Lemon and ginger tartlets flavoured with violets

The combination of the wonderfully evocative flavours of lemon, ginger and violets work together beautifully!

Sweet pastry

120g butter
75g icing sugar
2 egg yolks
250g cake flour, sifted

Lemon and ginger filling

5 eggs
200ml (¾ cup) castor sugar
45ml (3T) violet-flavoured icing
  sugar (*see* Cook's notes)
190ml (⅔ cup) melted butter
125ml (½ cup) fresh lemon juice
30ml (2T) finely grated fresh ginger
  (*see* Cook's notes)
30ml (2T) violet-flower water (*see*
  Cook's notes)
8 fresh violet flowers (petals only)

fresh violet flowers, for garnish

Serves 8

Sweet pastry

1. In a food processor or mixer, cream the butter and icing sugar.
2. Add the egg yolks, one by one, and mix until smooth and creamy.
3. Add the flour all at once, and mix until it just comes together.
4. Transfer the pastry to a sheet of cling wrap, shape into a ball, wrap tightly and place in the fridge to rest for 30 minutes.
5. Spray eight 9cm-diameter loose-based tart tins with a non-stick cooking spray.
6. Sprinkle some icing sugar on a clean work surface. Unwrap the chilled pastry, flatten slightly, roll out and divide into 8 pieces. Press the pastry evenly into the base and sides of each tin, making sure it is no thicker than 2mm. Trim the edges to neaten. Cover with cling wrap and rest in the fridge for 15 minutes.
7. Preheat the oven to 150°C.
8. Remove the pastry cases from the fridge, uncover and prick the bases with a fork.
9. Line each tart tin with baking paper (making sure the sides are covered), fill with baking beans and blind bake for 20 minutes. Set aside to cool (*see* Cook's notes).

Lemon and ginger filling

1. Preheat the oven to 180°C.
2. In a medium bowl, whisk the eggs, castor sugar and flavoured icing sugar together for 1 minute.
3. Add the melted butter, lemon juice and ginger and whisk for another 2 minutes, then leave to stand for 5 minutes. Skim off any foam that forms.
4. Pour the filling into the blind-baked pastry cases, and bake for 15 minutes.
5. Spoon over the violet-flower water and fresh violet petals and bake for another 5 minutes.
6. Remove from the oven and set aside on a rack to cool.

To serve

Remove the tartlets from the tins and garnish with a fresh violet flower.

COOK'S NOTES

- The pastry cases can be made up to 12 hours ahead, wrapped in cling wrap once cool, and placed in the fridge until required. Fill the tarts and bake them shortly before serving.
- Grate the ginger very finely to avoid ending up with stringy bits in the filling.
- Violet-flavoured icing sugar is available at speciality baking shops. To make your own, finely chop the petals of 4–5 violet flowers (*Viola odorata* or *V. cornuta*) and add them to 100g icing sugar. Store in an airtight container for two months, mixing once a week. Whizz to a fine powder in a blender before using. This is best if done in advance but, for immediate use, double the quantity of violet petals and blend straightaway.
- Violet-flower water: Pull the petals off 16 violet flowers and put them into a small bowl or cup with 30ml (2T) boiling water. Use a teaspoon to crush the petals to extract as much colour as possible.
- If you want to pick edible flowers from your garden, do not use any toxic insecticides or pesticides on your plants. (Ask your nursery or garden centre for advice on suitable products.) Never consume flowers purchased for the vase, as they may have been treated before or after picking to prolong their shelf life.

WINE SUGGESTIONS

Choose a wine with a zesty, minerally and lightly toasted character; a sparkling wine will be perfect.
- Méthode Cap Classique Blanc de Blancs (100% Chardonnay) from Stellenbosch, Western Cape.
- Franciacorta Riserva, an elegant, delicate sparkling wine from eastern Lombardy, Italy.

Index

Entries in **bold** denote photographs

A

abalone **30**, 31, **32**
agapanthus 59, **62**
alikreukel 86, 87
Aloe spp. 59, 175, **183**
Amaryllis belladonna 85
Artichokes with Hollandaise
   sauce **49**, 50
artisan chocolate 41
Asparagus purée 36
'Athene' rose **33**, 41, 147

B

baby sole 122, **123**
basmati rice 78
battonage 117, 131, 175
Beef, pan-fried fillet 166, **167**
beens, green **150**, 152
Beetroot and cardamon pap **90**, 92
beetroot juice 92
belladonna lily 85
biltong, shark 17
   venison 119
black mussels 148, **149**, **159**
blood flower 103, **116**
blue crane **28**, 29
bokkoms 176
boletus *see* mushrooms
Braemar House 12, **13**
Bread
   Focaccia 14, **15**
   mini loaves 148, 163
bunny chow 148
Burgundy 20, 85, 104, 181
Butterbean mash 34, 36

C

candied rose petals 41
Cape gooseberry custard 140
capelin caviar 122
Cape salmon 108, **109**
'Cape snow' 29, **32**
Carpobrotus spp. **120**, 129
Cauliflower soufflé **49**, 51
caviar, capelin 122
   seaweed 86, 87
ceps *see* mushrooms (boletus)

Chicken, turkey and game birds
   Breast of guinea fowl with
      olive and rosemary tapenade
      180, 181
   Chicken breasts baked in a
      lemon and anchovy butter
      sauce 34, **35**
   Roast turkey with sage and
      orange stuffing 64, **65**
   Roasted Stellenbosch quails
      with pancetta, black olive and
      honey stuffing **150**, 151
chincherinchee **19**
chocolate, artisanal 41
   mousse 41
Chardonnay-poached prickly
      pears 83
Chilled cucumber soup 75
Christmas decorations **58**
courgette flowers, stuffed 110, **111**
Cranberry and orange jelly 71
Cranberry and Pinot Noir sauce 66
crayfish 78, **79**
custard, Cape gooseberry 140

D

Desserts
   Fig and pistachio tart with
      Sauvignon Blanc sorbet 96, **97**
   Ginger biscuit ice cream with
      cranberry and orange jelly 71
   Honey panna cotta with
      Chardonnay-poached prickly
      pears **82**, 83
   Lemon and ginger tartlets
      flavoured with violets 186, **187**
   Hamilton Russell Vineyards
      Pinot Noir-poached pear
      brûlée tart **172**, 173
   Malva pudding with cape
      gooseberry custard 140, **141**
   Mango and lemon-scented
      geranium sorbet on lemon
      verbena shortbread **114**, 115
   Milk tart in cinnamon phyllo
      pastry cases with quince and
      rosehip cream **154**, 155
   Olive oil ice cream with sour
      fig syrup **128**, 129

   Rhubarb ice cream with rose
      meringues and mini toffee
      apples **24**, 25
   Rose geranium chocolate
      mousse **40**, 41
   Summer fruits in a white
      chocolate, almond and
      honey sauce 54, **55**

E

edamame beans 92
edible flowers, caution 41, 148,
   156, 182, 186
Eucalyptus spp. *see* sugar gums
everlastings 13, **19**, **32**, 43, 85

F

fallow deer sausage 132, **133**
figs 96, 98
Fish and seafood
   abalone **30**, 31, **32**
   alikreukel 86, 87
   Baby sole baked in a creamy
      lemon-shrimp sauce 122, **123**
   black mussels 148, **149**, **159**
   bokkoms 176
   Cape salmon 108, **109**
   crayfish 78, **79**
   Franschhoek salmon trout with
      kaffir lime oil **136**, 137
   Gnocchi with prawn and white
      mussel mayonnaise **60**, 61
   Kingklip with a parsley crème
      fraîche sauce **90**, 91
   Lemon-baked yellowtail **48**, 49
   Lime-marinated Cape
      salmon 108, **109**
   nori seaweed 86, 87, **158**
   octopus 44, **45**
   perlemoen *see* abalone
   prawn mayonnaise 61
   rock lobster *see* crayfish
   salmon trout **136**, 137
   seaweed caviar 86, 87
   shark biltong cream sauce 17
   smoked snoek chowder 163
   squid ink ravioli **16**, 17
   Walker Bay abalone done
      three ways **30**, 31

   Walker Bay black mussel
      bunny chow in a 'kooigoed'
      sauce 148, **149**
   Walker Bay crayfish with
      lemon, ginger and coriander
      sauce 78, **79**
   Walker Bay octopus served with
      three dipping sauces 44, **45**
   white mussels 61
   yellowtail **48**, 49
flowers, edible (caution) 41, 148,
   156, 182, 186
Focaccia 14, **15**
fynbos 29, 32, 43, 59, 73, **88**,
   103, 147, 161, 164, 175
fynbos honey **28**, 98

G

garlic, roasting 44
Ginger biscuit mix 71
   ice cream 71
gnocchi 61
guinea fowl **180**, 181

H

Haemanthus coccineus 103, **116**
Hamilton Russell Vineyards 6,
   7, **8–9**, 18, **42**, 76, 88,
   134, **161**
   cellar operations 13, 43, 59, 73,
      62, **84**, 85, 103, 117, 131,
      147, 161, 175
   Chardonnay 14, 43, 59, 66,
      83, **89**, 147, 161, 163, 176
   Extra-virgin Olive Oil 14, 20,
      31, 44, 49, 61, 64, 66, 78,
      91, 92, 104, 108, 110, 119,
      122, 129, 137, 148, 151,
      152, 163, 166, 168, 169,
      176, 181, 183
   Fynbos honey **28**, 54, 61, 78,
      83, 96, 98, **134**, 143, 151,
      156, 163, 181
   harvest **84**, 85, **88**, **89**, **91**, 103
   Pinot Noir 20, 43, 59, 66, 73,
      85, 104, 147, 161, 172
   pruning 12, 13, 161, **164**, 175
   tasting room **42**, **99**, **121**, **139**
   vines 12, **33**, 43, **59**, 131, **147**

vineyards 13, 29, **52–53**, 73, **88**, **93**, **103**, 117, 131, 147, 161, **174**, 175
Hemel-en-Aarde Valley 6, 7, **160**, 161
Helichrysum pandurifolium 59
   H. petiolare 50
Hollandaise sauce 50
honey, fynbos **28**, 98

I

Ice cream
   ginger biscuit 71
   mango and lemon-scented geranium sorbet **114**, 115
   olive oil **128**, 129
   rhubarb **24**, 25
   Sauvignon Blanc sorbet 96, 98
icing sugar, violet-flavoured 186

J

Japanese mayonnaise 31
Jasminum officinale 78

K

Kaffir lime oil 137
kingklip **90**, 91
Klein River Gruyere Cheese 51, 104, 138, 168, 176
'kooigoed' 50, 59, 148, **159**

L

lamb, peppered shoulder 20, **21**
Lampranthus furvus 73
   see also vygie
Lemon and ginger tartlets 186
Lemon-baked yellowtail **48**, 49
lemon-scented geranium 115
   sorbet **114**, 115
Lemon thyme mini-loaves 163
lemon verbena **107**
   shortbread 115
Lime-marinaded Cape salmon 108
Leucadendrons **164**
Leucospermum 28, **29**,

M

Malva pudding 140, **141**
Mango sorbet **114**, 115
mayonnaise, Japanese 31
Meat and venison
   biltong, venison 119
   Fairfield fallow deer sausage with porcini pap 132, **133**

Pan-fried fillet of beef with creamy horseradish sauce 166, **167**
Peppered shoulder of spring lamb with roasted baby vegetables in a Pinot Noir sauce 20, **21**
Ravioli of venison biltong and mushrooms **118**, 119
Milk tart **154**, 155
Mini toffee apples **26**, 27
mini-loaves 148, 163
mushrooms 104, 117, 119, 132
   boletus 104, 117, 119
   porcini pap 132
   powder 104
mussels, black 148, **149**, **159**
   white 61

N

nori seaweed 86, 87, **158**

O

octopus 44, **45**
olive oil 103, 117, 129
   ice cream **128**, 129
   see also Hamilton Russell Vineyards Olive Oil
olives **43**, **76**, **77**, 103, 116, **117**, 147
Olive and rosemary tapenade 181
olive vinaigrette 44
Opuntia ficus-indica **76**, 83
Ornithogalum thyrsiodes **19**

P

Pancetta, black olive and honey stuffing 151
panna cotta **82**, 83
pap 92, 132
Passiflora edulis **63**
Pasta
   Gnocchi with prawn and white mussel mayonnaise **60**, 61
   ravioli (making) 17, 86–87, 119
   Ravioli of alikreukel and seaweed in a chilli, lemongrass and coconut milk broth 86, **87**
   Ravioli of venison biltong and mushrooms in a creamy mushroom sauce **118**, 119
   Squid-ink ravioli filled with goat's cheese, in a lime and shark biltong cream sauce **16**, 17

Pastry
   phyllo cases 155
   sweet 96, 98, 172, 186
pear brûlée tart 172, 173
Pear and pomegranate sauce 173
Pelargonium citronellum 115
perlemoen *see* abalone
Phaenocoma prolifera 85
phyllo pastry cases 155
pine nuts **106**
Pinot Noir 20, 66, 104, 181
   -poached pears 172
porcini 119, 132
   pap 132
pomegranate **135**, 172, 173
prawn mayonnaise 61
prickly pears **76**, **82**,
   Chardonnay poached **82**, 83
proteas 28, **29**, 140, **142**, **143**, 147, 161
   Protea repens 131, 140, **142**, 143, 161
   Protea repens syrup 140, 143

Q

quails, roasted 151
quince **158**
   and rosehip cream 155
   paste 156

R

Ravioli, *see* Pasta
renosterveld 59, 159
Rhubarb ice cream **24**, 25
Rice
   Jasmine-scented basmati 78
   Mushroom risotto 104, **105**
   Waterblommetjie risotto with bokkoms 176, **177**
rock lobster, *see* crayfish
rocket, wild **106**, 108
'rooisewejaartjie' 13, **19**
Rose geranium chocolate mousse 41
Rose meringues **24**, 25
Rosehip syrup 156
roses **33**, 41, 59, 73, **77**
rose petals, candied 41

S

sage flowers **18**
Sage and orange stuffing 64
samp 138

Salads
   Rocket, sorrel, courgette, radish and pine nut 108
   Warm salad of multi-coloured chard and red onion 168
salmon trout **136**, 137
   see also Cape salmon
Sauces and accompaniments
   Chilli, lemongrass and coconut milk broth 86
   Cranberry and Pinot Noir sauce 66
   Creamy horseradish sauce 166
   Creamy lemon-shrimp sauce 122
   Creamy mushroom sauce 119
   Green olive vinaigrette 44
   Hollandaise sauce 50
   Kooigoed sauce 148
   Lemon, ginger and coriander sauce 78
   Lime and shark biltong cream sauce 17
   Olive and rosemary tapenade 181
   Pancetta, black olive and honey stuffing 151
   Parsley crème fraîche sauce 91
   Pinot Noir sauce 20
   Porcini cream sauce 132
   Prawn and white mussel mayonnaise 61
   Romesco-inspired sauce 44
   Sage and orange stuffing 64
   Sesame and ginger vinaigrette 44
   Sesame dressing 152
   White chocolate, almond and honey sauce 54
sausage, Fallow deer 132, **133**
Sauvignon Blanc 14, 17, 98, 108
   sorbet 96, 98
seafood, *see* Fish and seafood
seaweed 86, 87
   caviar 31, 86, 87
   nori 86, 87, **158**
Sesame dressing 152
sewejaartjies 13, 19, 29, **32**
   see also everlastings
shark biltong cream sauce 17
Sideroxylon inerme 75
Smoked snoek chowder 163
sole, baby 122, **123**
Sonderothamnus speciosus 174
sorbet, *see* ice cream

sorrel, wild 75, 163
Soups
   Chilled cucumber and wild
      sorrel 75
   Smoked snoek chowder with
      wild sorrel 163
sour figs **120**, 129
   syrup 129
Squid-ink ravioli **16**, 17
star jasmine 72, **73**
strawberries, wild 54
stuffing, sage and orange 64
   pancetta, black olive and
      honey 151
sugar gums 13, **42**, 73, **80–81**,
   146
Sugarbush protea 140
Suikerbos, *see* Sugarbush protea
Summer fruits 54, **55**
suurvye, *see* sour figs
Sweet pastry 96, 98, 172, 186
Sweet potato chips, roasted 66
Syncarpha vestita 29, 32

T
tapenade 181
Turkey, brining 64, 66
   roasting 64, **65**
Turnip and parsnip purée 182

U, V
Vegetables and side dishes
   Artichokes with Hollandaise
      sauce **49**, 50
   Asparagus purée 36
   Beetroot and cardamom pap
      with edamame beans **90**, 92
   Butterbean mash 34, 36
   Cauliflower soufflé **49**, 51
   Creamy pink peppercorn and
      cashew nut samp **136**, 138
   Deep-fried vine leaves 66
   Fresh asparagus 36
   Fresh green beans in a sesame
      dressing **150**, 152
   Jasmine-scented basmati rice 78
   Lemon-thyme mini-loaves 163
   Parisienne potatoes with

      flat-leaf parsley **150**, 153
   Porcini pap 132
   Potato, pea and fennel mash
      122
   Roasted sweet potato chips
      with chilli and ginger 66
   Rosemary-skewered roast
      potatoes 169
   Stuffed courgette flowers
      110, **111**
   Sweet potato chips 66
   Turnip and parsnip purée 182
venison
   biltong 119
   sausage 132, **133**
vinaigrette 44
vine leaves, deep fried 66
Viola odorata 182, 186
   V. cornuta 182, 186
Violet-flower water 182, 186
vygie 73

W
Walker Bay 6, **38–39**, **72**, **126–127**

Walker Bay abalone done three
   ways **30**, 31
Walker Bay black mussel bunny
   chow in a 'kooigoed' sauce
   148, **149**
Walker Bay crayfish with lemon,
   ginger and coriander sauce
   78, **79**
Walker Bay octopus served with
   three dipping sauces 44, **45**
Wasabi cream 163
waterblommetjies 176, **178**
Waterblommetjie risotto with
   bokkoms 176, **177**
White chocolate, almond and
   honey sauce 54
White milkwood berry syrup 75
white mussels 61
wild rocket **106**
wild sorrel 75
wild strawberries 54

X, Y, Z
yellowtail **48**, 49

CONVERSION TABLE		
METRIC/IMPERIAL	METRIC/IMPERIAL	METRIC/IMPERIAL
Teaspoons	Cups	Weights
2 ml – ¼ tsp	60 ml – ¼ cup	1 oz – 30 g
3 ml – ½ tsp	80 ml – ⅓ cup	2 oz – 60 g
5 ml – 1 tsp	125 ml – ½ cup	4 oz – 125 g
10 ml – 2 tsp	160 ml – ⅔ cup	8 oz (½ lb) – 250 g
20 ml – 4 tsp	200 ml – ¾ cup	16 oz (1 lb) – 500 g
	250 ml – 1 cup	2 lb – 1 kg
Tablespoons	375 ml – 1½ cups	3 lb – 1.5 kg
15 ml – 1 Tbsp	500 ml – 2 cups	4 lb – 2 kg
30 ml – 2 Tbsp	750 ml – 3 cups	5 lb – 2.5 kg
45 ml – 3 Tbsp	1 litre – 4 cups	
		Liquids
		1 pint – 600 ml
		2 pints – 1.25 litres
		3 pints – 1.90 litres
		4 pints – 2.5 litres

OVEN TEMPERATURES			
	°C	°F	Gas Mark
very cool	100	200	¼
very cool	120	250	½
cool	140	275	1
cool	150	300	2
moderate	160	325	3
moderate	180	350	4
moderate–hot	190	375	5
hot	200	400	6
hot	220	425	7
very hot	230	450	8
very hot	240	475	9

Thank you to

My wonderful husband, Anthony, for all his inspired ideas and support.

Miguel Chan, master sommelier extraordinaire, for his generosity in providing insightful

and varied wine recommendations for my dishes.

Jeanette Adams, my right hand in the kitchen and Hendrik Mouries, our vigilant gardener,

and the Hamilton Russell Vineyards team, for their years of support.

All my family and dear friends for their help, support and willingness to be my guinea pigs as I tested, tasted

and retested the recipes for this book.

Journalist Ronelle Terreblance and author Kerneels Breytenbach for introducing me to Random House Struik.

The team at Struik Lifestyle, Linda de Villiers, Helen Henn and Gill Gordon,

and photographer Sean Calitz, thank you so much!

Olive Hamilton Russell

Published in 2012 by Struik Lifestyle
(an imprint of Random House Struik (Pty) Ltd)
Company Reg. No 1966/003153/07
Wembley Square, Solan Street, Cape Town 8001 South Africa
PO Box 1144 Cape Town 8000 South Africa

www.randomstruik.co.za

ISBN 978 1 43170 092 9 print
ISBN 978 1 43230 122 4 epub
ISBN 978 1 43230 123 1 pdf

Publisher: Linda de Villiers
Managing editor: Cecilia Barfield
Design manager: Beverly Dodd
Designer: Helen Henn
Editor: Gill Gordon
Photography: Sean Calitz
Proofreader: Samantha Fick (Bushbaby Editorial Services)

Reproduction: Hirt & Carter Cape (Pty) Ltd
Printing and binding: Tien Wah Press (Pte) Limited, Singapore.